3
Vital
Questions

Transforming
Workplace
Drama

"As a Human Resources professional for over 30 years, I can attest that drama is the one constant reality in the workplace, regardless of industry, size of company, or intentions of leaders. I have witnessed the seismic shift that happens when a company commits to *The Power of TED* (*The Empowerment Dynamic)* and people choose to think about what we see, how we feel and why we behave as we do. David Emerald's *3 Vital Questions: Transforming Workplace Drama* empowers us to create healthy workplaces focused on dynamic interactions and sustainable results."

—**Karen M. Wall**, Vice President, HR Shared Services, Fresenius Medical Care—North America

"David Emerald is one of the great champions of positive behaviour change as the best remedy for the heavy cost of workplace drama – both personally and organizationally. His book, *3 Vital Questions*, provides accessible new insights and tools that will be valuable for anyone."

—**Michael Bungay Stanier**, author of the WSJ bestseller *The Coaching Habit*

"*3 Vital Questions* is engaging, easy to absorb, and packed with wisdom and actionable insights that can be implemented at every level of an enterprise. CEOs should make this required reading for everyone in their organization."

—**Rand Stagen**, Partner, Stagen Leadership Academy

"Creators change the world, but victims suck. They suck time, energy and momentum out of challenges desperate to become great opportunities. David Emerald has mastered helping leaders move from being victims of circumstance to creators choosing the brilliant futures they want. His new book, *3 Vital Questions* is the roadmap for how to make this happen."

—**Mike Maddock**, Founding Partner and CEO of Maddock Douglas, author of *Free the Idea Monkey* and *Plan D*

"This book illuminates the secret ingredient in change leadership—the human dimension. With its laser focus on outcomes, the *3 Vital Questions* will revolutionize the way you think, relate and act to create sustainable change in times of rapid transformation."

—**Alison L. Ferren**, MBA, Senior Vice President, Integration and Performance Improvement, Thomas Jefferson University & Jefferson Health

"The *3 Vital Questions* and TED* frameworks have given us a common language to build awareness with all of our stakeholders. Applying this approach has resulted in greater trust and increased decision-making speed, while empowering individuals at home as well as at work."

—**Dale Herold**, President, Distributor Operations Interstate Batteries

. . . .

Praise for *The Power of TED* (*The Empowerment Dynamic)*

"Really smart and helpful information about . . . stronger, saner, and healthier ways of behaving."

—**Elizabeth Gilbert**, author of *Eat, Pray, Love* and *Big Magic*

"The Empowerment Triangle is a highly original and effective escape from the Drama Triangle."

—**Stephen Karpman**, MD, originator of the Karpman Drama Triangle

"An engaging story that will help you escape from the traps of victimhood and enablement. Applying what you read will help you become truly proactive as you develop high trust in yourself and healthy relationships with others. Enjoy it and make the shift that creates true effectiveness!"

—**Stephen M.R. Covey**, bestselling author of *The Speed of Trust* and co-founder of Franklin Covey's Trust Practice

3
Vital
Questions

Transforming
Workplace
Drama

DAVID EMERALD

POLARIS

3 VITAL QUESTIONS
Transforming Workplace Drama

Published by

Polaris Publishing
321 High School Rd NE—PMB 295
Bainbridge Island, Washington 98110

FIRST EDITION

Cover Design by
Realistic Studio

Interior Design by
Lanphear Design

ISBN: 978-0-9968718-3-9

Printed in the USA

EDU036000 EDUCATION / Organizations & Institutions
EDU032000 EDUCATION / Leadership
EDU046000 EDUCATION / Professional Development

Dedication

To Donna Zajonc: wife, partner, TED* mom,
Co-Creator, Challenger, and Coach

List of Diagrams

Contents

Introduction

As the iconic band the Grateful Dead famously sang, "What a long, strange trip it's been."

I have been blessed by a career that began with a focus on interpersonal, team, and organizational communication. Through a series of fortuitous events, over thirty years ago I made the transition from public relations, employee newsletters, and speechwriting to leadership education, executive coaching, and organizational development. I began helping individuals, teams, and organizations learn how to collaborate in creating their desired outcomes and, in the process, learn to communicate more effectively with one another.

Along the way, I faced both personal and professional challenges fraught with drama. Divorce. Being fired from a job I didn't relish in the first place. Working for one of the worst bosses ever. You get the picture—the usual roller coaster of life. Of course, I have been blessed with many ups as well as downs on the journey.

Dealing with the dramas in my personal life, coupled with what I was learning in my profession, led to the writing and publication of my first book, *The Power of TED* (*The Empowerment Dynamic)*. Largely due to the struggles I faced in these personal dramas, the book was written as a fable on "self-leadership."

The fable format of that book struck a chord. To date, *The Power of TED** has sold well over 100,000 copies in print, e-book, and audio. People continue to write me to share how the book has changed their relationships at home, at school, and at work. I have been humbled by the stories people have told in their letters and emails. Some have brought me to tears.

To my surprise and delight, many organizations started adopting *The Power of TED**, its language, and its frameworks in their efforts to improve the ways employees relate to one another, as well as to customers and other stakeholders.

As an outgrowth of the reception *The Power of TED**was having in organizations, I began teaching classes—along with my wife, Donna Zajonc, who is a Master Certified Coach and a great facilitator. We developed and now teach the 3 Vital Questions as a way to more clearly and directly apply the TED* (*The Empowerment Dynamic)® frameworks to organizational realities.

As Donna and I began to offer the 3 Vital Questions® material via workshops, consultations, and presentations, we found that simply asking these questions engaged people and contributed to significant positive change in their workplaces. People began asking, "When are you going to write the 3 Vital Questions book?"
Well, here it is.

The Cost of Drama in the Workplace

If you have ever experienced infighting, such as a team or a department pitting itself against another team or department; if you have ever worked for a micromanaging and overbearing boss; if you have ever navigated the changes that come with a merger or other significant restructuring process, then you have had a front-row seat to organizational drama.

The cost of drama is tremendous, for any organization. Do a quick online search on "the cost of workplace drama" and you may be amazed at some of the hard dollars-and-cents costs associated with organizational conflict. These costs accrue due to lost productivity, turf battles, infighting, gossip, rumors, picking sides, blaming, faultfinding, absenteeism, turnover, and engaging in what Peter Block has called the politics of manipulation.

Gallup research indicates that there's approximately $500 *billion* in lost productivity annually, in the United States alone, due to negative behavior in organizations. Other research has estimated that managers spend as much as 40% of their time dealing with conflict and drama. Sadly, in the case of some organizations, that estimate may be low.

At a minimum, workplace drama causes inefficiency, frustration, and waste. The personal costs to those who work in organizations is immeasurable.

At one point in my career, a new boss took over the department I worked in. This person, I soon discovered, was the most drama-producing boss I would ever work for.

Every night I went home stressed and exhausted, worrying what the next day would bring. I tossed and turned at night. I wasn't present to my family even when at home because I was always thinking about my problems at work. I engaged in "ain't it awful" stories of my work life with anyone who would listen. This book's fable turns that story around, eradicating the drama in much the way I wish I had been able to turn my own story around those many years ago.

The Problem with Our Approach to Change

Needless to say—but its very prevalence points out our need to say it—drama is one of the primary forms of resistance and reactivity that hobbles the rate of positive organizational change. Even when positive change does take place, the initial atmosphere of success and freshness can quickly turn into an atmosphere of failure and discouragement once the drama resumes. And almost any experience of drama at work can be traced back to the impact of resistance to change.

What is the answer? Transforming and reducing drama in the workplace.

Before I get into that story, however, I think it is important to reveal the deeper professional context that gave rise to this work.

This book was more than three decades in the making. Since it is entitled *3 Vital Questions*, I guess you could say it represents one vital question per decade!

Over that period, I was working in leadership education

and development, executive coaching, and organizational development, and in this work I found countless models, workshops, books, articles, and conversations that informed me along the way.

Life in our organizations is undergoing unprecedented and increasing change. A bold new era of volatility, uncertainty, complexity, and ambiguity (sometimes referred to as VUCA) presents constant challenges for leaders and organizational cultures. Ask any executive—whether in the corporate, nonprofit, or educational world—and they can readily describe the anxiety that comes with this volatile mix of conditions.

In my professional journey, there was one pivotal learning experience that sparked the inquiry—and set the stage—for what became the 3 Vital Questions.

It was the mid-1990s. I was attending a workshop on organizational culture. I was there in my capacity as program manager and internal organizational development consultant focusing on executive education for a major financial services corporation. One of the faculty (David Ulrich of the University of Michigan's Ross School of Business) presented his research findings on the success rate of change efforts in organizations. I was stunned (but not too surprised) when he reported that 80% to 85% of change efforts fail to produce their intended results!

Other studies' results have landed in the same ballpark as Ulrich's findings. At best, research indicates at least 60% of organizational change efforts fail to produce lasting positive change.

To be fair, the studies included a range of "failure"—from crash-and-burn utter failure to the change initiative simply taking longer than planned or not attaining the level of results (e.g., cost savings) originally projected.

My own experience had shown me that many change initiatives bring with them a certain level of resentment, resistance, and (surprise!) drama—themes that are woven throughout this book.

But first, back to the impact of that learning experience and those statistics. I started to wonder: what might be some of the underlying causes of such a poor success rate? I pondered, did a little research, had conversations with colleagues. And then . . .

Then, I came across an article by Peter Senge ("Building Learning Organizations," published in the March 1992 issue of the *Journal for Quality and Participation*). Embedded in the article was the clue I had been searching for—one that has informed much of my work ever since.

Senge referred to an observation by Douglas Englebart (collaborative work expert and inventor of the computer mouse), that every organization has three dimensions of work. Every organization—be it a for-profit corporation, a nonprofit organization, an educational organization, or any other type of entity.

The article referred to these three dimensions simply as A, B, and C (see also Diagram 1):

The production and delivery of products and/or services. This is "the work" we engage in to serve our customers and clients.

The design and implementation of the systems, processes, and structures that enable the work to be done. The primary responsibility for this dimension is held by *management.*

The way we think about how we think, interact, and take action. To quote Senge's article, "Ultimately, the quality of [this] work determines the quality of the systems and processes [that organizations] design and the products and services [they] provide" (p. 35). This is the work of *leadership*—which can include anyone, anywhere in the organization.

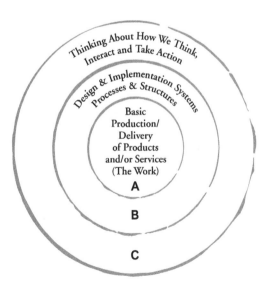

Diagram 1. The Three Dimensions of Work

Here's an example of how dimension C affects dimension B that is critical to the epiphany that is coming:

Douglas McGregor, at MIT's Sloan School of Management in the 1940s, developed a theory of employee motivation that addresses thinking about how we think, interact, and act. He called it, simply, Theory X and Theory Y.

Theory X sees employees (and co-workers) as problems. It assumes that people are basically lazy and will avoid work if they can, so they need to be controlled and threatened with punishment if they do not perform. This, of course, creates environments of mistrust, blame, and drama. This set of assumptions leads to systems, processes, and structures (dimension B) that are traditionally controlling, hierarchical, heavy on policies and procedures, and perpetuate an environment of "us" versus "them," such as workers versus management, "our" department versus others, and so on.

Theory Y, on the other hand, assumes that employees and co-workers are inherently self-motivated and seek out work and responsibility that satisfies their desire to create products and services that meet the needs of others. They want to do a good job. Therefore, management seeks ways to tap into the creativity and commitment of those doing the work (dimension A) through systems, processes, and structures (dimension B) such as self-directed work teams, employee empowerment initiatives, encouragement of employee input and feedback, and so on.

The Epiphany

I still remember reading that article and having one of those eureka moments as it suddenly hit me why so many change efforts fail.

And here it is, the fundamental reason: most change initiatives are rooted in dimension B—management's systems, processes and structures—without any consideration for, let alone work within, dimension C, which is how we're *thinking* about how we work.

Managers may restructure or implement systems for improvement, or attempt to instill what some call a "burning platform for change" in the workforce. None of these are bad things to do per se. In fact, in the right context, they can be hugely useful. But if they are initiated without stepping back into dimension C—thinking about *how we think, how we interact,* and *how we take action*— then sustainable and successful change is quite unlikely. As one former colleague quipped, "All we're doing is pushing soap around the tub!"

The 3 Vital Questions are purely focused on dimension C—a dimension of work that has been missing in all too many change methodologies. And while this book is squarely focused on organizational life, the challenge of creating change in our personal lives (e.g., weight loss, healthy eating, smoking cessation) also can be addressed by stepping back and doing dimension C work on ourselves.

It begins with establishing and practicing the 3 Vital Questions, which set the stage for sustainable change and fulfilling work. It is this inside-out work (on the individual and personal level) that leads to outside-in work on the organization.

The 3 Vital Questions® (3VQ)

The following questions represent my addition to the contributions of many others. The questions focus on what I have found to be the *most* important frameworks and tools that inform dimension C—the essential dimension that precedes as well as enhances successful change management. I believe these three questions are what change *leadership* is all about.

Question 1. Where are you putting your focus?
Are you focusing on *problems* or on *outcomes?*
Question 2. How are you relating?
How are you relating to others, to your experience, and even to yourself? Are you relating in ways that produce or perpetuate *drama*, or in ways that *empower* others and yourself to be more resourceful, resilient, and innovative?
Question 3. What actions are you taking?
Are you merely *reacting* to the problems of the moment, or are you taking *creative* and generative action—including the solving of problems—in service to outcomes?

In formulating this set of 3 Vital Questions, I have benefited greatly from the influence of intimate and distant mentors, as well as a measure of creative thinking and experience. In particular, I was blessed many years ago when three powerful influences came into my life in a synchronous way over a period of several months.

First, I was exposed to the work of Robert Fritz, through his early course on the Technologies for Creating, which I experienced through a workshop facilitated by a certified instructor. The principles of what Fritz calls structural tension are captured in his books *The Path of Least Resistance* (1989) and *Creating* (1991). Fritz's concepts were described as creative tension in Peter Senge's classic *The Fifth Discipline* (1990). I choose to describe this framework—in chapters 10 and 11—as *dynamic tension* because my experience is that it characterizes the constant change and unfolding involved in the process of creating outcomes. This work informs the third of the 3 Vital Questions.

Shortly thereafter, I was introduced to Bob Anderson, founder of The Leadership Circle (www.theleadershipcircle.com) and now chairman and chief development officer of the Full Circle Group (www.fcg-global.com), as well as co-author with William Adams of the extraordinary book *Mastering Leadership* (2016). I cannot overstate Bob's influence on me, through his genius and through our work together over the past quarter century (plus), during which Bob became a close colleague, mentor, collaborator, and ultimately a dear friend. I was fortunate to become an early facilitator of his Empowering Leadership workshop (a title later changed to Mastering Leadership and now called Authentic Leader).

Bob's originality and creativity have led to an amazing body of work, including the most powerful 360-degree feedback tool I have ever experienced: the Leadership

Circle Profile. Bob's early work on mental models and what he calls the human operating system forms the foundation of the 3 Vital Questions. In particular, it informs the first of the 3 Vital Questions and the way I describe the two primary orientations (which I refer to as the Problem and Outcome Orientations and he refers to as the Reactive and Creative Orientations). References to the Leadership Circle Profile (LCP) come from my former work as a facilitator of certifications for the LCP and my continued services as a coach and debriefer of this most powerful feedback system.

Shortly after meeting and beginning to work with Bob, I entered a challenging personal period in which I learned about the Karpman Drama Triangle, developed by Dr. Stephen Karpman in the late 1960s. His brilliant observation of the relationship dynamics that show up whenever we experience or witness drama was, for me, a blinding flash of the obvious. After months of contemplating the insights of this model, I experienced the epiphany of a much more empowered way of being in relationship with others. This "aha" moment eventually led to the writing and publication of *The Power of TED* (*The Empowerment Dynamic)*.

While writing this book on the 3 Vital Questions, I drew on specific concepts learned from two other particular sources: The idea of there being a "commitment behind the complaint"—discussed in chapter 8—comes from the work of Robert Kegan and Lisa Laskow Lahey, presented in their book *How the Way We Talk Can Change the Way We Work: Seven Languages of Transformation* (2001). The distinction between the "looking good" and "learning" intentions—mentioned in chapter 9—comes from the work of Diana Cawood (www.cleardaycoach.com) and is used with permission.

These frameworks and relational "technologies" are the heart and soul of this book. Though I have read, experienced, and experimented with countless theories, workshops, models, and tools over the years, in my teaching over the past thirty years I have returned again and again to the foundational questions that are presented here.

In keeping with *The Power of TED**, this book is written as a fable in which people in different areas of an organization learn to apply the 3 Vital Questions as they navigate change in ways that empower them, transform their workplace dramas, and produce lasting positive results.

You will meet Lucas, a young professional in an informal leadership role, who is marking time in a job that no longer inspires him while dealing with a new boss who adds fuel to his struggles.

Staying late one night, Lucas meets a custodian by the name of Ted. But Ted is no ordinary custodian. These two strike up a conversation that unfolds over many months as Ted shares with Lucas the 3 Vital Questions that he learned years before from a senior executive.

Besides sharing what he is learning with his wife, Sarah, Lucas discovers that his neighbor, Kasey, is a successful middle manager in another part of the same organization and that, earlier in her career, Kasey once had much the same experience with Ted-the-custodian that Lucas is now having. Kasey becomes a mentor to Lucas, helping him to think through and, most importantly, apply the 3 Vital Questions to the challenges he faces.

Lucas discovers that in work, as well as in all areas of life, transformation begins by recognizing one's own drama. And so his story begins.

VITAL **1** QUESTION

Where are you putting
your focus?

CHAPTER ONE

Late Night at the Office

....

With a sizzle and a flicker, the light above Lucas's desk went dark.

"Great," he muttered to himself. He sat back, looked around his cubicle, and caught sight of the time on his laptop. "Seven o'clock and here I am—again! I'd be sitting down to dinner with Sarah and the kids right now if I didn't have to redo this report for one of my data analysts to submit to our new boss. No way around it, though. This thing has to be on his desk first thing in the morning, and I've got to make a good impression." Lucas paused, then, "I've heard he can be a real pain when things aren't perfect," he whispered to nobody.

His mind started racing, running through the list of reasons he felt so anxious. First off, his job as a team lead of Customer Service Department analysts in this financial services megacorporation was no longer satisfying. "I'm tired of dealing with data all the time," he thought, "and leading a group with no real authority can be frustrating. But this job does pay the bills."

The worries mounted. Here he was at age thirty-six, with a mortgage on a house in a nice kid-friendly neighborhood. He had an awesome marriage and two great kids—a son in first grade and a daughter in third. But already he and Sarah were talking about how to save for their kids' college tuition, though it would be five more years before his own student loans were paid off. It helped that Sarah had begun working part-time at a daycare center once the kids were in school. Lucas and Sarah had decided together, when they became parents with Emily, that Lucas would be the primary breadwinner, and now he was feeling the pressure of that decision.

Meanwhile, at work, two of the four people on his team just didn't seem to get it when it came to writing reports. But Lucas didn't have the authority to hire, fire, or discipline them, so he was always having to double- and triple-check their work. His new boss had a reputation for being a perfectionist and quick to fly into a rage.

"No wonder I'm so stressed," Lucas said out loud, and he let out a huge sigh.

"Sorry to hear that, young man," came a voice from the next cubicle.

Somewhat startled, Lucas said, "Sorry, I didn't think anyone else was here."

"Just working my way down the corridor," the custodian said, appearing at the entrance to Lucas's office. Leaning against his cleaning cart, the man introduced himself. "Greetings. My name's Ted. I'm new on this floor—used to work a few floors up. Now that Sally's decided to retire and play with her grandkids, though, it'll be me cleaning up around here nights. So if you generally work late like this, I guess you'll be seeing more of me."

Ted glanced up and noticed Lucas's light was out. "Do you like working in semidarkness, or could you use some illumination? I know some people do see their computer screens better when it's not so bright."

"Oh, I could use some illumination, all right," Lucas offered as he also gazed up at the darkened ceiling.

"Okay then, give me a couple minutes. I'll head down to the supply closet and be back in a jiff," Ted said with a smile.

"Don't bother," Lucas said. "I can finish this report at home tonight."

"No bother at all, young fella," Ted replied. "I see my job as maintaining an environment where you and your colleagues can do your best work. So I'm more than happy to help shed some light on things." Ted smiled, with a sparkle and a wink, then turned and headed down the corridor.

Lucas smiled to himself. "Sure seems friendly," he thought, "and sure doesn't seem like any other janitor I've talked to before." He turned his attention back to his computer and the report he was rewriting.

A few minutes later, Ted was back with a small ladder and a light bulb. "I can replace that bulb from the cubicle next door to yours," he said.

The walls of Lucas's module were only a few feet high, and in a moment, Ted's head popped up over the partition as he reached to retrieve the burned-out bulb.

"I appreciate you taking the time to do that," Lucas said. "I assumed someone would take care of it tomorrow.

I didn't know Sally was retiring. She was nice, but I don't recall her saying much when I worked late. Have you worked here very long?"

Ted unscrewed the light bulb. "Oh, I've been here seven or eight years now, but I've been a custodian all my adult life. May sound strange, but I love my job. I like being of service in maintaining the work environment. If you don't mind me asking, what has you working late this evening? Important project?"

Lucas sighed and told Ted about the report he was editing and the early-morning deadline. As the new bulb brightened, Lucas blinked and squeezed the bridge of his nose. "I have to admit, it's not the first time I've had to fix someone else's work—not by a long shot."

Ted listened with interest. Still holding the old bulb, he gave it an affirming wag. "Yep. Before you knew I was here, I believe you said something about being stressed."

"That's only the tip of the proverbial iceberg," said Lucas, surprised at his own candor.

"Yeah, I can imagine," said Ted. "I've seen lots of different workplaces over the years, and it seems like folks are getting more and more stressed all the time. A few have told me their work is more complex than ever, and on top of that, they're more uncertain about the future than they've ever been."

"Nailed it," said Lucas.

Ted came back around to the entrance to Lucas's cubicle as he folded up his stepladder. "I feel fortunate that I've also had the pleasure to see a few places where people are truly excited about their work, where folks are creative and full of fire. There's a whole different feeling about those places, I can tell you."

Lucas sighed again. "That sounds so different from the aura that seems to prevail around here. I'd love to hear about those other workplaces!"

Ted nodded as he picked up Lucas's trash can. "I worked at this one place that was really something. I was employed by this service that assigned me to a consulting company. Turned out I got the chance to have some interesting chats with the CEO. I even came to find out his 'secret sauce' for engaging the people who worked there. It was a marvel how resourceful and creative folks were at that company, even though—just like here—everyone seemed to be dealing with challenges and changes. Ended up it all came down to just a few important questions."

Ted set down the empty trash can. "Well, nice talking with you. Don't believe I got your name?"

"Oh! It's Lucas. Hey, sometime I'd really like to hear what those questions are, if you wouldn't mind."

"Not that I want to encourage you to work late, Lucas, but we can talk a bit more when I do see you again. Next time our paths cross, I'd be happy to take a few minutes to share what I've learned. I'll tell you, those questions have made quite a difference for me over the past ten years." Ted reached for the handle of his cart. "Maybe there's a good reason I got transferred to this floor."

With that, Ted began wheeling the bin down the corridor, humming softly to himself.

Lucas turned back to his computer. For the next half-hour he alternated between focusing on the editing he had to do and wondering what in the world those questions were. He clicked Save on the report and looked at the time. "Great! If I leave now, I can be home in time to tuck the kids in."

Lucas packed up and put on his coat. He glanced up at the brand-new light overhead, smiled, and headed for the elevator.

CHAPTER TWO

Where Are You Putting Your Focus?

Once again Lucas found himself sitting in front of his computer as those around him left for the day. In the cubicle behind his, he heard someone call out, "You're not making this a habit, are you, Lucas? You'll make us all look bad!"

"No, I'm heading home in a few more minutes," he answered absently, staring at the remaining fifty or so emails in his inbox. He knew he needed to wade through them and respond. His new boss had made this nonnegotiable, imposing a "twenty-four-hour rule." All client emails, internal or external, now required a response within one day's time.

Lucas texted Sarah to tell her he had to stay a little late, but that he'd be home in time for dinner with the family.

He knew the drill all too well, even if he had risked leaving this task to the end of the day. As he had guessed, a good percentage of the messages were emails that were FYI (for information only) and could be quickly filed or deleted. Luckily, none of the other emails required more than a quick reply or an attachment of an existing document to fulfill the request. The process was moving along nicely.

As Lucas approached the last few emails, he heard a door open in the distance, along with the sound of humming. He looked at his watch. He had been hoping for another opportunity to ask Ted about those "few questions" he had mentioned when they first met, a little over a week ago.

Lucas was just wrapping up his last email reply—Whew! It had taken only a moment to send the monthly data on customer service wait-times to one of his internal clients— when, over in the next cubicle, he heard Ted emptying the trash can.

"Is that you, Ted?" Lucas reached over to shut down his computer for the night.

"One and the same." Ted chuckled as he finished dusting and tidying up the desktop of the cubicle next door. "That sounds like Lucas keeping night hours again!"

Ted pushed his cart up to Lucas's office.

Lucas replied, "Yeah, there's always more work. Somehow I always have more left to do at the end of the day. I just finished a load of emails I had to respond to before I leave." Lucas glanced at his computer as it finished shutting down. "Ted, I really enjoyed our conversation the other night. And I'm still curious about those questions you mentioned."

Ted checked his watch. "Well, if you've got a few minutes before you need to go, I could briefly share the first question with you. I figure it'll take about fifteen to twenty minutes."

Lucas leaned back in his chair and smiled. "Perfect! If I leave here within a half-hour, I can still get home in time for dinner with my family."

Ted glanced around. Lining the walls of the corridor running the length of the cubicles were a series of whiteboards. The one across from Lucas was blank. "You mind if I draw a few diagrams on the board there?"

"Not at all," said Lucas. "I have some markers in my desk here—you can use these." He pulled open a drawer and pulled out three colored markers. He handed them to Ted.

"Mind if I sit down?" asked Ted.

"Please do," said Lucas, pointing to the guest chair next to his desk.

"There are actually three vital questions in all. Your answer to the first one will reveal how you see and operate in the world. According to many others I know who have taken this question to heart, it has changed the way their internal environment affects their behavior. And that, in turn, has transformed their relationships at work, at home . . . in so many aspects of their life.

"Are you ready for it?"

"Bring it on." Lucas leaned in with a smile.

"Here it is," said Ted. "*Where are you putting your focus? Are you focusing on problems or are you focusing on outcomes?*" He raised an eyebrow and waited.

"No doubt about it," said Lucas. "All we seem to talk about around here are problems and what we're going to do about them."

Ted smiled. "Good for you! You just outlined the Problem Orientation, which is one of two primary orientations. The CEO I mentioned said that the Problem Orientation is the default mindset of most people and organizations. But that's getting ahead of ourselves.

"There's an organizing framework behind this first vital question that I need to share before we go any further. Guess you could say I am going to toss you a FISBE."

"Toss me a Frisbee?" Lucas asked.

Ted made a "just a minute" gesture with his finger, got up from the chair, and stepped out into the corridor. On the whiteboard he drew three circles connected by arrows, forming a sort of loop. Above it he wrote: *FISBE.*

"Nope, it's a FISBE, not a Frisbee," he said with a chuckle.

Lucas maneuvered his chair to get a better look at the board.

"FISBE is an acronym that describes the human operating system that every one of us is using, all the time," said Ted. "The *F* in FISBE stands for *focus*," he said, writing the word in the top circle, "and this focus sets up the rest of the operating system. That's because whatever you focus on, that's what gets your inner state going. Your inner state is your emotional response to whatever you place your attention on—what you're thinking about. So the *I* and *S* stand for *inner state*." Ted added *IS* to the second circle in the diagram.

"Depending on this emotional response," he continued, "this inner state then drives your behavior." He wrote capital *BE*, for behavior, in the third circle. "So FISBE stands for *focus, inner state*, and *behavior*. Got it?"

Lucas looked at the board for a minute and thought it over. "I get the diagram and how the focus leads to an

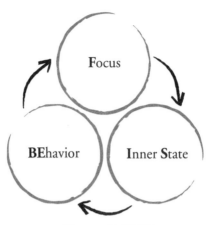

Diagram 2. FISBE

inner state that drives behavior. But why do you call this the human operating system?"

"Good question! Because," Ted continued, "as my CEO friend pointed out, we human beings are *cognitive*—or thinking—creatures. Our thoughts set up our focus. We're also *emotional* beings. Our emotions determine our inner state. And, of course, as individuals and groups, we take actions and engage in *behaviors*," Ted explained.

"Hmm," said Lucas, squinting at the diagram.

"Your FISBEs—you could also call them mindsets or orientations—have everything to do with how you move through your day and, ultimately, your life. Your primary FISBE drives your behavior, just like the operating system drives that computer you just turned off.

"So here's where it gets really interesting, Lucas. In the same way you can upgrade the operating system in your computer, you can upgrade your internal operating system as a human being."

"Interesting analogy," Lucas said. "I'm listening."

"Let me share an example of how different FISBEs, or operating systems, can change our experience. Are you game?" Ted leaned against the whiteboard, glanced at the diagram, and crossed his arms.

"Absolutely!" said Lucas.

"So," Ted said, "here in the Pacific Northwest, we love our beaches. Imagine you're walking along the beach and it's a beautiful sunny day. The water of Puget Sound is smooth and lapping gently on the shore. Not far offshore, you see a sloop gently sailing by. Got the picture?" Ted asked.

Smiling, Lucas said, "Sure do!"

"Now let's assume there are two different people walking along that same beach. One of them looks out at the sailboat and recalls happy memories from childhood when her family often had fun playing at the beach and occasionally going out on a neighbor's boat. Her inner state is one of happiness and contentment. So, she stops for a moment, smiles, and takes a deep breath, enjoying the salt air." Ted paused.

"See her FISBE, Lucas? Her focus is on pleasant memories triggered by the boat, her inner state and emotions are positive and serene, so her response—her *behavior*—is to pause and drink in the moment."

"Makes sense," said Lucas.

Ted continued. "Now the other person walking on that beach looks out over the water and sees the same sailboat gliding by. His focus goes to a time in childhood when he and his family were out on a boat and he fell overboard and nearly drowned. His heart starts beating faster as he feels the anxiety and fear of that experience all over again. He turns and quickly walks away from the shore and heads toward the parking lot.

"You can see how the same situation triggered positive thoughts for one person and negative thoughts for the other—their focus was different. This caused them to experience very different inner states, which then led to very different actions, or behaviors. The same situation, with different FISBEs, created two totally different experiences."

"Interesting," mused Lucas. "Do those two different examples illustrate the two orientations you mentioned earlier?"

"You're a quick study, Lucas!" Ted turned to the whiteboard and drew two more loop diagrams.

The Problem Orientation

Above one diagram, Ted wrote: *Problem Orientation.*

"This and the other FISBE is called an orientation. That just means whatever you put your focus on—your orientation—is what sets the whole operating system in motion. This first one, the Problem Orientation," Ted said, pointing to the board, "is your default orientation as a human being, as I'm sure you'll quickly see." Ted paused with a wink and turned back to the board. "It's also the one you said is so common around here."

"As you might suspect, the focus here is on problems," he said, and he wrote *Problem* in the focus circle. "A problem can show up in all kinds of ways: maybe someone emails you, or calls or texts you. Or maybe someone walks into your office and starts talking about a problem. "As you take in this new information as a problem," said Ted, "your inner state arises—and that's going to be some kind of anxiety." Ted wrote *Anxiety* in the inner state circle. "Then, depending on how bad you think the problem is, your anxiety could be anything from a little irritation to intense fear. Either way, the inner state of anxiety will trigger you into action.

"This action you take—that's your behavior, of course— is some form of reaction. There are four ways you might react: fight, flight, freeze, or appease."

"It sounds pretty dramatic," Lucas said.

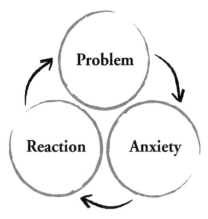

Diagram 3. The Problem Orientation

"It sure can be! At least until you start to see what's happening in your FISBE," said Ted. "You might *fight* the situation in some aggressive way, to try to protect yourself. Or try to get away—take *flight*, like a bird escaping a barking dog. Or maybe you're not sure how to react, so you do nothing—you *freeze* and hope the problem goes away. Last of all, you could react by playing nice and trying to *appease*, or smooth things over. Whichever way you go, you are caught in a reaction," Ted concluded. Then he wrote *Reaction* in the behavior circle.

Ted stepped back and regarded his handiwork. "So you see, here in the Problem Orientation, you focus on problems, which turns on your anxiety, and that drives a reactive behavior. Sound familiar?" Ted asked.

Lucas leaned back in his chair and let out a deep sigh. "Wow. You just described what it's like almost every day around here!"

"Can't say I'm surprised." Ted shook his head. "It's what I've seen in most of the companies I've been around. The Problem Orientation seems to be the main operating system within us as individuals. And it's the main way we relate with others as well. That's why my CEO friend called it the default orientation."

"I can see that," said Lucas. "It's kind of discouraging, though."

"Only if you don't know you're doing it!" said Ted. "Once you start noticing it, things look a lot more hopeful."

He scratched his ear. "There's something deeper here, though," he went on, "that I should caution you about.

Embedded in this orientation, there's a false assumption and a false hope."

Ted paused and faced Lucas. "Let me ask you something. When you're faced with a problem around here and your anxiety flares up, what do you tell yourself you're reacting to—the problem or the anxiety?"

"The problem, of course!" Lucas quickly answered.

"See, there's the trick!" exclaimed Ted. "That's the false assumption."

Lucas frowned.

Ted continued, "You're telling yourself you're reacting to the problem, when really you're reacting to the anxiety you feel *about* the problem. If you didn't feel some level of anxiety, you'd let the situation pass on by. The false assumption is that the problem is *driving* this operating system. But it isn't—the Problem Orientation, the operating system, only sets it in motion. It's actually your *anxiety* that's driving the whole shebang." Ted chuckled, looking over his drawings.

"Wow, I can see that," Lucas agreed. "I'm not sure what to make of it, but I see what you're saying."

"There's one other thing you have to be careful of," Ted added. "There's a false hope underlying this whole way of being, too." He raised an eyebrow. "The false hope is that if you can just solve the problem, then everything will be okay . . . or that you'll then be able to focus on something more important. Right?"

"Of course. That makes sense to me. Why would that be false?" Lucas said.

"Well, let's see. You said the Problem Orientation describes your experience of your typical workday. So let me ask you something else." Ted crossed his arms. "Say you're lucky enough to solve a problem—what typically takes its place?"

Lucas didn't have to think long. "Another problem. Seems like there's always a new issue lurking under the last one. I'm just waiting for the next incoming problem!"

"And that's why it's a false hope that problems will go away," Ted responded, and he uncrossed his arms. "As long as you're working in this operating system—the Problem Orientation—then for every problem you seem to solve, another one will pop up in its place. It's like that old game of Whack-A-Mole, where as soon as you get rid of one nuisance critter, another one pops up."

Lucas shook his head and was silent for a few seconds. "Yeah, it's a downer," was all he could think to say. "A false assumption and a false hope. But both of those ring true to me."

"I know what you mean," said Ted. "So, can you see why you need an upgrade from this operating system?" he asked, pointing over his shoulder at the Problem Orientation FISBE.

Lucas leaned forward and said, "I really do, Ted. No joke. Would you please, please show me a better way to work?"

"And live," Ted added with a smile. "Sure thing."

The Outcome Orientation

Turning back to the whiteboard, Ted wrote *Outcome Orientation* above the second diagram.

"I think you're going to find this one a little easier to stomach," he said. "It's a lot more positive, for one thing, and it may feel more familiar than you'd expect. I'm sure you've had some experience operating from this orientation, at least from time to time."

In the focus circle, Ted wrote the word *Outcome.*

"In this orientation, you have a much different focus. Here your thinking is oriented toward envisioning an outcome. Sometimes the outcome you have in mind is clear—you know almost exactly what it is and how you want it to happen. Other times this outcome may be somewhat vague in your mind, but you have a general idea of the direction you're heading.

"What's important is that you *care* about the outcome you envision. Because when you really care about it, that ignites an inner state of passion," said Ted, and he wrote the word *Passion* in the inner state circle. In the behavior circle he wrote *Baby Step*, then turned to face Lucas.

"That passion," he continued, "provides the motivational fuel to take the next step in your process toward creating the outcome—whatever that step may be.

"So, in the Outcome Orientation here, the behavior is referred to as a baby step. Because the action you take is usually something that happens little by little, step by step. It could be as small as making a phone call or doing some research or . . . really anything that's the next step in your process of creation. I could say more about the idea of baby steps, but let's save that for when we get into the third vital question."

"Sure," Lucas said. He laughed. "My brain is pretty full already! But I'd like to understand the Outcome Orientation a little better."

Diagram 4. The Outcome Orientation

Ted chuckled. "It always makes me laugh when I say thank you to someone and they say 'No problem.' Shows how common the Problem Orientation is in our culture. But, to your question . . . Let's see, can you think of a time you were operating from this Outcome Orientation?" he asked.

"Hmm, let me think," Lucas began. "A time I was focused . . . on an outcome that I cared about and then took some baby steps to accomplish. Yeah—got it! Finishing my computer science degree." He took a breath.

"Sarah and I were married then," Lucas said, "and we knew we wanted to start a family, but I wanted a college degree that was marketable and could support us. I really cared about that—doing everything I could to help take care of my family—though I'm not sure I was all that passionate about computer science. But that's another story.

"Anyway," said Lucas, "I was working as a waiter at a decent restaurant, taking classes at night and working my job schedule around daytime classes while Sarah worked as a nanny for a family with a toddler. She had already completed her associate's degree in early childhood education, but she wanted a job with flexibility so we could work our schedules around each other's. Sarah was a rock—she really supported me in juggling it all. I guess you could say that every class I took was a baby step."

Lucas glanced at his desk, at the framed picture of Sarah and the kids. "I feel so lucky and supported by Sarah to this day," he said. "We love being parents, and I learn a lot from her—and *with* her."

"Great example, Lucas!" Ted chimed in. "While you and Sarah were working through your degree, you were plugged into this Outcome Orientation operating system, and you didn't even know it. The key to this first vital question is to upgrade to the Outcome Orientation as your primary way of thinking, here at work and, really, throughout your life."

Ted looked at his watch. "Got a few more minutes? I could point out a few differences between these two orientations, if you have the time and interest."

Lucas looked at his phone and scratched his chin. "Let me text Sarah and ask her if she minds holding dinner for another fifteen minutes. I'll tell her I have something very interesting to share with her when I get home. That'll get her attention."

The AIR of the Work Environment

As Lucas was texting Sarah, Ted turned and wrote the word *AIR* on the board between the two FISBE diagrams. "Speaking of attention, Lucas," he said, "that's one of the differences here, between the Problem Orientation and the Outcome Orientation. AIR stands for three major distinctions between the two FISBEs: your *attention*, *intention*, and *results*. You'll see these two operating systems have very different 'airs' about them." Ted smiled as he made the air quotes.

"As I said, the *A* here stands for *attention*," he said, pointing to the board. "Here in the Problem Orientation, your attention is on the problem, of course. When this is your default way of being, you go through your day focusing on the things you *don't want* and *don't like*—which is why you call them problems. You're almost always scanning your environment for what's wrong or what's not working—or you're on the lookout for another nuisance critter to pop up."

"Have you been following me around?" Lucas chuckled. "That is exactly how my days seem to go lately."

"Well, as you adopt the Outcome Orientation and start to use that operating system more consistently," Ted said, "your attention begins to move naturally toward whatever it is that you *do want*, and what you really care about. That doesn't mean you won't have any more problems, but it does mean there will be a big shift in your relationship to those problems. Instead of seeing problems everywhere you look, you start taking on *only* the problems that need to be solved to create the outcome you want. And that brings us to the *I* in AIR—which stands for your *intention*.

"But first I have a question for you, Lucas."

"Sure," said Lucas.

"In the Problem Orientation, your intention is to get rid of, or get away from . . . what?" Ted asked.

"The problem!"

"You got it, but if this was a game show, you would lose a point there!" Ted shook his hands in the air and laughed. "That was actually a trick question. Remember the false assumption I mentioned?"

"Oh yeah," Lucas said. "The assumption is that I'm reacting to the problem itself, when really I'm reacting to the anxiety I feel about the problem. Is that it?"

"Smart fella." Ted nodded. "Your intention is really to get rid of, or get away from, your anxiety through various behaviors—either fight, flight, freeze, or appease. Behaviors you hope will solve the problem. But, as we've already said, it's the anxiety that is really the driver in this problem-focused operating system. And in just a minute you'll see why that is.

"But first, look at intention in the Outcome Orientation. When you operate from here," said Ted, pointing to the

Outcome Orientation FISBE, "your intention is to move toward the outcome and, through the baby steps, or the actions you take, to bring that intention into being over time."

Lucas joined in. "So, the difference is between *moving away* from what you don't want—the problem—and *moving toward* the outcome you do want."

Ted grinned. "Yep!"

"That's great, Ted," said Lucas with a smile. "So, the *A* stands for attention, and the *I* stands for intention. Tell me again what the *R* stands for?"

"Ah, now you're going to see why these two operating systems are so very different," said Ted as he turned back to the whiteboard.

Below each of the FISBEs, Ted drew what looked like a backward *L* lying on its side. Alongside the short vertical line, he wrote *Results*. Below the longer horizontal line, he wrote *Time*.

"Here's the real whopper between these two orientations. Over time, they lead to two very different patterns of *results*."

Diagram 5. Results Over Time

CHAPTER THREE

The Predictable
Pattern of Results

Ted faced Lucas. "Let's look at how each orientation—problem-focused or outcome-focused—leads to a different pattern of results. It's amazing that these patterns are so predictable, but it's true. You can test the orientations and see the results for yourself.

"I'm going to lead you through each part of each FISBE. First, look at the Problem Orientation FISBE. When a problem occurs, what happens to your anxiety? Does it increase or decrease?" Ted asked.

Lucas thought for a moment. "Generally, it increases—it goes up."

"Right," said Ted. "So let's put a plus sign, like this"—and he drew a + on the whiteboard—"here between *problem* and *anxiety* to show that when a problem occurs, anxiety increases. Now, as your anxiety increases, what happens to your tendency to react to the problem?"

"I guess that's going to increase, too," Lucas answered. Ted drew another plus sign, this time between *anxiety* and *reaction.*

"Now pay close attention to this next part. If your reaction is helpful and affects the problem in a positive way—if the situation gets better—then what happens to the intensity of the problem? Does it increase or decrease?"

Lucas paused. "Well, if the situation is getting better, then I assume the intensity of the problem goes down. It decreases."

"Bingo!" said Ted, raising his marker triumphantly. "Which is why we place the minus sign"—which he duly wrote on the whiteboard—"between the reaction and the problem. This is crucial: the action you took had a positive impact on the situation, so the intensity of the problem actually decreased.

"Now watch this. As the intensity of the problem goes down, anxiety decreases." Ted drew another minus sign to show anxiety decreasing when the intensity of the problem decreased.

"And remember," Ted continued, "the real motivation for your reaction is *not* the problem—it's the anxiety. So, as the anxiety goes down, your tendency to react to the problem decreases, too." Ted drew another minus sign between *anxiety* and *reaction*, showing less energy going into the reaction.

"When you keep reacting to a problem without ever really solving it—when you just shift your attention to the next incoming problem—eventually the problem resurfaces, often with more intensity. Then the anxiety goes back up." Ted drew the final plus sign on the diagram, between the reaction and the problem.

"So there you go, Lucas," he continued. "As the intensity of that problem goes up again, the anxiety goes up, and once again we try to do something about the problem.

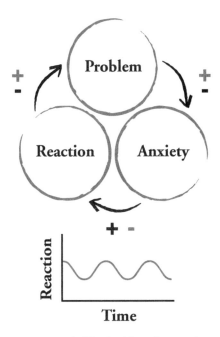

**Diagram 6. The Problem Orientation
and the Roller Coaster of Results**

The pattern just perpetuates itself. It's a roller coaster of results that repeats itself time and again, for as long as the Problem Orientation is operating."

"Wow, Ted!" exclaimed Lucas. "Now I see what you mean about anxiety driving the operating system. At least I think I do."

Ted added, "So anytime you find yourself faced with a situation that seems to come up over and over again—be it with a team member at work, someone in your personal life, or even within yourself—it is virtually guaranteed you're coming at that situation from the Problem Orientation. You do something about the situation, it gets better for a while, and then sometime down the road, there it is again!

"I'll bet you can think of an example of this roller-coaster pattern—maybe in a situation here at work?" Ted asked.

Lucas thought for a moment, then leaned forward. "Yeah, I had a situation like that with one of my team members last year. His performance just did not match the requirements of his job. It wasn't that he didn't meet objectives—because he did. It was the way he went about serving our clients. They would complain to me about his attitude and approach, and then as a result, he and I would talk, and he would agree with what the client expected. I would actively coach him, his performance would improve for a while, then, admittedly, I'd let the coaching slide, only to find myself having a very similar conversation six months later—the same cycle of activity all over again."

"Excellent example! Do you see the pattern of action and inaction there?" Ted asked, and he pointed to the graphic. "At its best, the pattern of results is this fluctuating wave. As long as you feel anxiety, you'll be in motion. However, as things start to get better, you actually lose your energy for action. You only engage in action when you're experiencing the things you don't want or don't like.

"And here's a key point. Don't be fooled into thinking this is a *problem-solving* mindset. It isn't. It is only a *problem-reacting* orientation. You think it's the problem that's causing you to act, but it's really the anxiety. So when the anxiety goes away you lose energy for action. And there you can see the impact of that false assumption we were talking about."

"That makes a lot of sense." Lucas looked at his watch. "Speaking of anxiety, I'm going to need to shove off in just a few minutes," he said. "I'm guessing the Outcome Orientation is associated with a different pattern?"

"It is," Ted agreed. "You see a totally different pattern of results. In the Outcome Orientation, the process is positive all the way around the FISBE." He pointed to the parts of the diagram as he spoke.

"As you focus on your envisioned outcome, your passion goes up." He drew a plus sign. "As your passion increases, your desire to take the next baby step increases, too." Another plus sign. "Then, as you take that next step, you get closer to, or clearer about, the outcome"—a third plus sign on the board—"and that increases your passion and your will to take action."

Ted went on: "You can look at this pattern of effectiveness as a growth curve." On the L diagram, he drew an upward curve showing increasing results occurring over time.

"Reality is rarely so neat and tidy, though. It's not usually an upward trend of continuous progress. When you're working toward creating your intended outcome, the process more often looks—and feels—like two steps forward, one step back." Ted drew a squiggly line across the upward curve.

"But even in those times when you feel you're taking one step back, if you stay focused on your envisioned outcome, that experience can give you important information for moving forward. In this orientation, you take many, many action steps—large and small—and over time, the outcome takes shape.

"Each step you take is going to get you closer to, or clearer about, the outcome. Nothing you do is neutral. With each step, you are either getting closer to, or further away from, what it is you want to accomplish. So it's critical to keep your attention focused on the outcome. If you do, then even what seem to be mistakes and setbacks can be important steps toward that desired outcome."

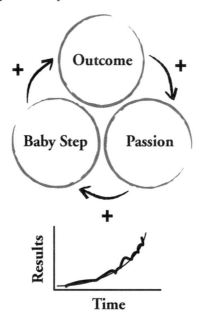

Diagram 7. The Outcome Orientation
and the Growth Curve of Results

The Problem With Problems

Ted gestured toward the board with his marker. "One last point about these two orientations," he added. "While you were figuring out how you'd get your degree in computer science, did you face any problems?"

"Absolutely!" said Lucas.

"That's the problem with problems—they do exist," said Ted. "Stuff happens. Problems are a natural part of creating any outcome. It's important to remember this— and then to actively engage in solving the problems that get you closer to your envisioned outcome.

"In the Problem Orientation, you unwittingly allow circumstances to define your focus by giving your attention to whatever is generating anxiety. You've heard the expression 'the squeaky wheel gets the grease'? That's a snapshot of the Problem Orientation, too. A lot of time and energy is wasted causing other folks to feel anxiety, in the hopes that a jolt of anxiety will get them to pay attention to certain agendas or needs."

Lucas interjected, "Again, I have to say . . . it sounds like you work around here all day, not just at night!"

"Problems define the focus in so many workplaces. But in the Outcome Orientation, you cultivate a very different relationship with problems. Because you have a vision of the outcome you want to create, you're able to pick and choose which problems really deserve your attention, focus, and energy. Then you can prioritize— dealing only with the problems most likely to help create that outcome. Anxiety may still be there, but you're no longer driven to react to it." Ted set down the marker at the whiteboard.

"In the Outcome Orientation, you actually start to seek out problems and welcome them as necessary steps to take in creating your desired outcome. The problems you solve along the way fuel your passion and enthusiasm about what you're creating. You know that solving any problems you face are getting you closer to, or clearer about, your ultimate goal."

Lucas looked at his watch and made a face. "Speaking of problems, if I don't leave now, Sarah is definitely going to react to my being late!"

Ted smiled. "I apologize. I've taken up more of your time than I should have. I'd better get going, too. I have a few more rounds to do tonight."

"Oh, don't apologize, Ted," said Lucas. "All of this has been incredibly helpful. If this is only the first of those three vital questions, I can't wait to hear the other two!"

"Time enough, my friend. I'm sure we'll run across each other again one of these evenings," said Ted.

Lucas grabbed his phone and stood up to get a full view of the whiteboard. "I have to take a picture of all this," he said. "I want to remember everything you've shared with me. I want to show it to Sarah when I get home."

As Lucas took a few shots of the whiteboard, Ted asked, "Do you ever write in a notebook or a journal?"

"I have a journal," said Lucas. "Last year I took a beginning leadership class offered by the company, and they gave us a journal as part of the class." Lucas slipped his laptop into his backpack, adding, "It's been a long time since I wrote anything in it, though."

"I see." Ted smiled as he took the handle of his cart. "You might want to think about pulling out that journal again and jotting down some of what we talked about tonight. And maybe print out and paste in that picture you just took as well. There'll be plenty more where that came from."

With that, Ted headed down the corridor, humming a bright tune.

Lucas took a good look at the picture on his phone, willing it into his memory. Then he headed out the door, eager to get home and tell Sarah all he had learned.

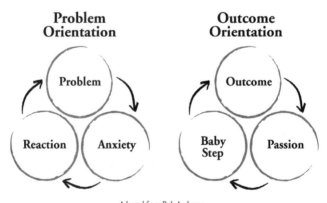

Adapted from Bob Anderson
The Leadership Circle—www.theleadershipcircle.com
Used with permission

Diagram 8. The Two Primary Orientations

CHAPTER FOUR

Discovering a Co-Creator

The next morning, Lucas pushed through the revolving door into the lobby of his office tower feeling grateful that Sarah had been so understanding about his being late for dinner. He had been so absorbed in recalling his conversation with Ted that he hadn't even called to tell her he was on his way home. It wasn't like him to forget that.

Sarah had met him at the door with a kiss and a smile and only said she had started to worry about him. Then she pulled dinner out of the oven—a dinner that had been keeping warm a little too long. He apologized as the kids scurried to sit down and chow down.

Once the whole family had sat down to dinner, he wanted to share his excitement about his conversation with Ted, but he realized it just wasn't the time. Instead he turned the dinner table conversation to its usual focus— Carson's and Emily's days at school and Sarah's adventures at her daycare center. Lucas always enjoyed hearing their day's news.

After they had cleared the dishes and gotten the kids into bed, he noticed Sarah was in a quiet mood.

"Sometime in the next few days I'd love to share with you what Ted and I were talking about today," he said.

"Sure, honey," said Sarah as she dropped into her favorite chair and picked up the novel she was reading. "I'd like to hear about it sometime." And they settled into their evening, Lucas feeling relieved that his showing up late for dinner hadn't soured Sarah on what he was learning from Ted.

The bright lights of the bank lobby brought Lucas back from his reverie. He made his way through the throng of people arriving for work. As he approached the elevator, he recognized a woman waiting there. She was one of his neighbors.

Lucas and Sarah bought their home a little over a year ago. It was in a family-friendly development, and they were still meeting and learning about the others who lived there. He remembered meeting this woman at the neighborhood Fourth of July picnic. He wanted to say hello, but what was her name? Lucas remembered discovering that they both worked at the same financial services company, but it had been a fleeting conversation, and he couldn't recall much more. As he neared the elevator, he thought, "Was it Kate? Kelley? Seems like it started with a K."

As the elevator door opened, Lucas said, "Hi! You live in Northtown Woods, don't you?"

She smiled as they, along with several others, stepped into the elevator. "Yes, I do," she said. "I think I met you and your wife and kids at the last neighborhood picnic." She put out her hand to shake. "My name's Kasey, and please remind me, you are . . . ?"

"Lucas," he said, relieved. "If I remember correctly, you work here at the bank as well."

"Yes, I do. Those picnics are so hectic, with all the activity and chitchat going on. I didn't have a chance to ask you—what do you do here?" she asked.

"I work in a support team for the Customer Service Department. I'm a team lead of a group of data analysts," Lucas said.

"Interesting," said Kasey. "I used to manage a customer call center until about a year ago. How do you like what you're doing?"

Lucas was a little surprised by her question, but since she was a neighbor, he decided to be more forthcoming than he might have been. "It's okay. Actually, it's a little on the tough side just now. I have a new boss who's making a lot of changes. And I have some challenges with a couple of my analysts." He paused, then quickly added, "But I really like the company."

"I think I know who your new boss is, so I can relate." Kasey said, with a wink that indicated she knew the elevator was no place to name names. "If I can be of any help as you work through your challenges, let me know, neighbor. The only advice I would give right now is to stay focused on outcomes and not get caught up in seeing your new boss—or even the challenges of change and your team—as problems to react to. Someday not too far from now you may look back on all of it as a great learning experience."

Lucas blinked, slightly stunned to hear these echoes of Ted's language.

"You okay?" Kasey asked.

"Uh, yeah . . . sorry," he stammered. "It's just . . . your advice sounds so much like a conversation I had with the custodian on our floor just last night."

Kasey brightened. "That wouldn't happen to be a guy named Ted, would it?"

"Wow! Yes, indeed!" Lucas beamed.

Just then the elevator door opened, and Kasey put her arm out to hold it. "Do you have a minute to finish this conversation in the hallway? I have to say, this is quite coincidental."

Lucas and Kasey stepped out of the elevator and into the foyer.

Kasey continued. "A couple of years ago, Ted was the custodian on our floor—we had some really amazing conversations. Has he said anything to you about the 'three vital questions' he picked up from a CEO he used to work for?"

"Yes!" Lucas said excitedly. "In fact, he shared one of those questions with me just last night. It's very interesting stuff." Glancing at his watch, Lucas realized he needed to get upstairs to his team. "Could we have coffee sometime, Kasey? It would be great to hear more about your experience with Ted."

"Sure thing—I'd enjoy that," Kasey said. "Just let me know when."

Lucas was thrilled at the thought of talking with someone who already had experience with what he was learning from Ted. "There's no time like the present," he thought.

"How about this afternoon or tomorrow morning?" he said aloud. "I have a team huddle this morning, and a meeting tomorrow afternoon, but . . ."

Kasey smiled warmly. "Another interesting coincidence. I got a text on my way in this morning that an all-day meeting I was supposed to have today has been postponed. What time would you like to meet—at Starbucks on the mezzanine?"

"Three o'clock?" Lucas offered.

"Three it is!" Kasey said. "See you then."

Lucas smiled broadly. "Great!" He stepped toward the elevator and pressed the Up button.

Custodian in Every Sense of the Word

Before heading to coffee that afternoon, Lucas took a few minutes to search for Kasey's name on the bank's intranet and learn a bit more about her. He assumed she was in her midforties and, given the floor she worked on, that she had a position of considerable responsibility. At the neighborhood picnic, Lucas had noticed Kasey's two children, young teens, playing amiably with the younger neighborhood kids.

He found that Kasey worked as a district vice president for retail banking and was responsible for all the banking centers in the downtown and surrounding areas, as well as all the retail banking call centers. "Pretty big job, with all those center managers reporting to her," Lucas thought. He also saw that she was, as she had said, the former manager of the Customer Service Department's credit card customer call center, a couple of floors above his. Lucas remembered that Ted had mentioned being reassigned from another floor in the high-rise building where they all worked.

Kasey was a fairly recent graduate of the bank's executive leadership development program for high-potential talent. Apparently her time in customer service had been her last rotation in the program. She had then graduated from the two-year process into her current position, about a year ago.

Lucas also discovered that the person Kasey had last reported to was none other than his new boss. "No wonder she knew who I was talking about." he thought, leaning back in his chair. He glanced up at the light above his desk and admired its bright new bulb, courtesy of Ted.

Lucas got up, grabbed his journal, and made his way down to the coffee shop. At this time of day it wasn't very busy—only a few people working on laptops as they took in an afternoon boost of caffeine. He stepped up to the counter and ordered an iced chai tea. For some reason he had lost the taste for coffee in the afternoon. He took his tea and sat in a booth toward the back where he could see Kasey when she walked in.

He was thinking how interesting it was that this conversation was about to take place. Lucas was certainly respectful of Kasey's position in the organization, but what he really wanted to talk about was her experience with Ted. He looked up just as she walked in, and he waved to get her attention.

Kasey waved back, held up her finger to say "Just a minute," then went to the counter and ordered a latte. While it was being made, Kasey came over and slid into the booth across the table from Lucas.

"I'm jazzed to talk with you about your experience with our mutual friend, Ted," she said.

"So am I," replied Lucas. "I can't wait to hear what the other two vital questions are."

Kasey laughed. "Sorry, neighbor, no spoilers! It'll be so much better—and more fun—if you get those directly from Ted. And I could never do justice to all of the three vital questions over coffee. But I'll be happy to meet up again and share some of the ways I've applied those questions as you learn more from him."

Lucas took a sip of his iced chai and said, "Okay then. Sounds like Ted's unique delivery of the three vital questions is going to be an important part of this."

"Absolutely! Direct experience is the best," Kasey responded.

"Interesting that he works as a janitor," Lucas said.

Kasey heard the barista call her name and rose to get her latte. "He's much more than a janitor, Lucas. He's a custodian in every sense of the word. Ted is a guardian of the wisdom he has accumulated from decades of keen observation—and a caretaker of conversations like the one he just started with you."

Kasey retrieved her latte and slid back into the booth. Taking a small sip, she continued. "Ted has absolutely shifted the way I think, how I relate with others . . . even how I plan things and when and how I take action. What I learned from him has dramatically upgraded the way I lead my team—and the way they lead their teams, because I've shared Ted's approach with them, too. What Ted teaches, or, I should say, shares from his experience, helped me see that everyone is actually a leader in both their work and their life."

"Hmm," Lucas said. "It sounds like you're talking about leaders besides the ones listed on the organization chart, like you. I know you oversee a group of banking center managers who lead the staff at their banking centers, as well as the retail call center."

"That's right, Lucas. We don't want to confuse managers with leaders." She took another sip of her latte. "Managers are, just as you say, people whose names appear on an org chart. But *leadership* has nothing to do with rank and position. Everyone can lead in their area of contribution or expertise. One of the maxims I learned from Ted is, 'Every job can have either a trivial description or a noble one.'"

Lucas nodded. "I remember Ted saying, when I first met him, that he was a custodian. He didn't use the word *janitor*. He told me his job is to be a custodian of the work environment."

"Oh, he's a custodian all right." Kasey smiled. "As I'm sure you'll see, the work environment he looks after goes well beyond the physical surroundings!"

Lucas said, "I am definitely intrigued, and I have to go in about thirty minutes. I'd love to hear more about your experience with that first vital question, the one about where you're putting your focus."

Thoughts, Feelings, and Actions

"This first vital question really sets the stage for everything else Ted's going to tell you," Kasey said, leaning back in the booth. "I feel fortunate that I met him several months before moving into my new role. During that time, we had the chance to talk quite a bit about some of the deeper applications of those questions."

"I'm all ears," said Lucas with a smile.

"One evening, Ted and I were talking specifically about the Problem Orientation and how what really drives that mindset is the anxiety or fear that comes with it. Did he go into that with you at all?" Kasey asked.

"Yes, he did. And I could see right away that when I focus on problems, my anxiety rises up and leads me to react."

"There were a couple of exercises Ted asked me to do that I found really helpful," Kasey continued. "I think we could cover them in a half-hour. Are you game?"

"Sure!" Lucas took out his journal and pen.

"The first exercise has to do with the thoughts and feelings you experience . . . and the actions you take . . . in each of the orientations. And just a note about 'thoughts'—they can be things you say silently to yourself as well as things you say out loud to other people," Kasey explained. Lucas wrote "thoughts, feelings, and actions" down in his journal.

"Okay, think of a time when you were clearly in the Problem Orientation." Kasey paused.

"Easy," Lucas said. "Two times, actually. First was in the huddle with my team this morning, when a couple of folks were goofing around and not taking the meeting seriously. And the other was last week in my one-on-one with my new boss. I believe you used to report to him?"

"I did. Now, keeping both of those situations in mind, what were some of your thoughts—things you said either to yourself or out loud?" Kasey asked.

Lucas thought for a moment. "'What a waste of time' was a thought that came up for me in both instances. In the huddle I remember thinking, 'These guys are so immature. It's so unfair that I'm expected to get them to perform even though I'm not paid as a manager.' And with my boss, I often say to myself, 'Why did I have to end up with this new boss? He seems to want to change everything we do, and he's so . . .'" Lucas hesitated a moment. "So controlling."

"All right," said Kasey. "So, how did you feel in those two situations? What emotions came up? What was your inner state, as Ted calls it?"

"Oh boy," said Lucas. "Frustrated. Even angry. With my team, we were meeting in the corridor, and I was embarrassed, thinking someone would see them goofing around. With my boss, I felt, well . . . really anxious, even scared. I was afraid to say something wrong that he might come down on me for saying."

"Okay," responded Kasey, "and then what did you do? In reaction to those emotions, what were your behaviors or actions?"

Lucas leaned back in his seat. "I finally showed my frustration to the team. I told them to stop acting like frat boys and listen up. I think my frustration was pretty obvious. With my boss, though, I sort of withdrew. I only said the minimum and let him do most of the talking. I've already learned there's no point in offering my ideas, because he'll just tell me why they won't work or how he has a better idea."

Kasey nodded. "Yeah, I know how that feels. We can talk more about your relationship with him another time, since we only have a few more minutes right now."

"I'd appreciate that," said Lucas, "but you're right, it can wait."

"You've made a good start on identifying your thoughts, feelings, and actions during those times when you're in the Problem Orientation. When you get a chance, you could also reflect on a time when you were operating from the Outcome Orientation—I can guarantee you'll notice you had more empowering, outcome-oriented thoughts at those times, and much warmer feelings. When you're engaged in service to outcomes you care about, even solving problems can bring you a sense of fulfillment and accomplishment.

"Oh! And there's one more exercise Ted had me do. It's about identifying reactive triggers and reactive strategies," Kasey said.

Reactive Triggers and Reactive Strategies

Lucas turned to a fresh page and wrote those words at the top. "What do you mean by reactive triggers?"

"A *reactive trigger* is anything or anyone that causes or activates you to react—to see that person or thing as a problem that engages some form of anxiety. Once you're triggered, you react with a fight, flight, freeze, or appease response. Those are the reactive strategies. I assume Ted mentioned those to you."

Kasey continued: "Personally, I can get triggered in meetings when someone interrupts me. Depending on the situation, my reactive strategy might be to confront the person in some way—a fight reaction—or I might withdraw and shut down—a form of flight. The reactive behavior is a strategy to try to control the anxiety you're feeling. Does that make sense?"

"I think so. When I get triggered, then I react from one of the strategies I've developed to try to control whatever is going on," Lucas said.

"You've got it!" said Kasey. "Take a minute and think about the kinds of people or situations or environments that usually trigger you to react."

Lucas sat back in his seat, sighed, and quickly responded, "My team and my boss, for starters, and I guess I already shared the strategies I use with them." He paused a moment. "Home can be pretty chaotic at times, especially when the kids have friends over and I've had a hard day at work. My strategy is to retreat to my little study and read or something."

Lucas added, "This is really interesting. I'm not sure I've ever stepped back and reflected on what triggers me, let alone what my reactive strategies are."

"The key, once you notice you've been triggered," said Kasey, "is to pause—I call it 'hitting the Pause button'—so you can shift away from reacting to what you don't want. That way you'll eventually make a more empowered choice."

Kasey checked her watch. "Hey, our time is about up. Just keep noticing when you get triggered and want to react—and sometimes you will. And keep track of what you do. That will help you discover your reactive strategies."

"This has been so helpful, Kasey," Lucas said as he closed his journal and slid his pen into the spiral binding. "You've helped me think a lot more deeply about what Ted told me. I can't thank you enough."

As she gathered her cup and napkin, Kasey pointed at Lucas's journal and said, "I think it's great that you have a journal to capture your thoughts and observations. Being able to step back and reflect on things is really key, Lucas. Ted calls it 'going up to the balcony.' The more you can observe, the more you will be able to make different and more empowering choices about how to respond. It will be great to get into the habit of writing down your observations of thoughts, feelings, behaviors, and actions, as well as your reactive triggers and reactive strategies."

As they stood up to leave, Kasey paused and said, "One more thing, Lucas. Whenever the opportunity presents itself for you to hang out and talk more with Ted, it's going to be, well . . . a learning experience that could change your life. Not just at work but at home, too. It changed just about everything for me!"

VITAL 2 QUESTION

How are you relating?

CHAPTER FIVE

How Are You Relating?

A week after Lucas met Kasey for coffee, he was still thinking a lot about both his time with Ted and the exercises Kasey had shared with him.

One evening at home, Lucas kissed the kids good night and left Sarah to tuck them in. Lucas assumed that Sarah would unwind from the day as she usually did, with her latest novel on loan from the library, and he decided to retreat to his study for a little while. Taking out his journal and pen, he began capturing some thoughts from his time with Ted and his coffee break with Kasey.

"It's surprising how much of the time I default to the Problem Orientation," Lucas wrote. He listed a few ways he had caught himself reacting to things recently. Just that morning, he had been in a staff meeting with his fellow customer service team leads. His boss was running the meeting. As Lucas listened to different people speak, he realized how often he heard whatever was being said—especially when his boss was saying it—as some kind of problem. He would then react to the perceived problem, at least in the privacy of his mind.

Just then, Lucas heard a light tap on his study door.

"What are you up to in there?" said Sarah, peeking into the study.

He motioned her in. "Pull up a chair."

Then Lucas did his best to describe what Ted had taught him. He showed Sarah the FISBE diagrams—how a person's focus engages their inner state, and how their behavior proceeds from that. He showed Sarah the diagram of the Problem Orientation FISBE with its focus on problems, anxiety, and reacting. Then he showed her the Outcome Orientation FISBE that leads to taking small empowering actions one at a time—actions Ted had called baby steps.

Sarah listened with interest. "I could use this stuff myself," she concluded. "When do you think you'll have a chance to learn more from this guy?"

"I really don't know," said Lucas. "It's kind of a spontaneous thing. I hope it's not too long, though. I'm already knee-deep in what he's taught me so far, and I want to learn more!"

Sarah smiled and nodded. She seemed as curious as Lucas to hear what else Ted would have to say.

For the next couple of weeks, Lucas was working on a project that filled his afternoons with meetings. He still hadn't seen Ted, and he was anxious for the next lesson. So one morning, Lucas checked in with Sarah to make sure she was okay with him staying late, on the off chance that he and Ted might connect. Sarah had enthusiastically agreed. "Anyway, it's about time the kids had another pizza night," she said. Then added, "Of course, if you do meet up with Ted, I expect you to fill me in."

"It's a deal."

That night, Lucas finished reading a report from one of the members of his team and smiled when he realized there was very little editing he needed to do. Just as he clicked Save on the document, he heard a door open down the corridor and the unmistakable humming of a gentle tune.

Standing up, Lucas peered over the wall of his cubicle and said loudly, "Good evening, Ted! When you make your way down to this area, I'd love it if we could visit for a bit."

"Absolutely, young man!" said Ted with a big smile. "Nice to see you! Should be coming by there about ten minutes from now."

"Great!" Lucas pulled his journal out of his backpack. These days he always kept it nearby in case he wanted to capture some insight or observation. He looked through the dozen or so pages he had filled since his coffee with Kasey.

Lucas had to chuckle at one entry he'd written just a few days ago. It described how he had returned to his desk from yet another long meeting, sat down, and clicked Download on his email. As he watched the twenty or so emails stacking up before his eyes (he'd only been away from his desk for an hour). Lucas noticed his anxiety rising and realized he was seeing every email as a problem to react to.

As he continued reading his journal, he saw that there had been many times recently when he had caught himself in the Problem Orientation and noted his feelings of anxiety along with his resulting reactive behaviors and actions. It was a little discouraging to see how often he had engaged in that pattern. But on a positive note, he had been taking Kasey's advice to also reflect on his experience anytime he noticed he was operating from the Outcome Orientation.

It was interesting how many of his reactions started with a single email. And what a big difference it made when he focused on the outcome as he made his way through these essential communications.

One recent email was from a senior manager who had criticized a report submitted by one of Lucas's team members. Reading the critical comments, Lucas had felt himself tensing up. There was an immediate, strong impulse to *do* something—anything—to dispel his anxiety. He could either forward the email to the author of the report and add his own criticism, or reply to the senior manager's email and defend his teammate.

Instead, Lucas had paused. He had asked himself, "What outcome do I want here?" In the end, he wrote an email to the senior manager and copied his teammate—the email asked for more information about what kind of outcome the manager had wanted that the report had not addressed. As Lucas read this journal entry, he recalled how relieved and even joyful he had felt when the senior manager's reply came back saying that, overall, the report provided good information, but one area had not been covered as specifically as it could have been. The senior manager even apologized for not stating clearly what he needed in the report! Then he spelled out in some detail how the report could be expanded to better meet his criteria.

What a savings in time, energy, and drama. In the past, Lucas might have spent a lot of effort reacting to the feedback, instead of focusing on how best to address the issue. When he focused on the outcome he wanted, the action he needed to take just seemed to present itself naturally.

Lucas skimmed through a few more of his journal entries. He noticed that, as Kasey had predicted, his thoughts had grown much more positive.

Many of his reflections had an "I can do this" quality about them. As he had written about his feelings and emotions, he had used upbeat words like *optimistic, empowered,* and *energized.* And Lucas noticed something else, too:

The actions he took when he was in the Outcome Orientation were different from the reactions he took when he got caught up in the Problem Orientation. At those times when he focused on the outcome, Lucas found himself more often collaborating with others, coming up with fresh ideas, and even taking risks to speak up. Of course, it had been a lot easier to speak up with his previous boss than it was now.

It surprised Lucas to realize that he actually enjoyed solving problems when he simply viewed them as barriers to the outcome he wanted to accomplish. He also noticed that from the Outcome Orientation, he dealt with mistakes and setbacks differently, making well-considered choices about how to move forward.

Lucas was lost in reflection when Ted rolled his cleaning cart up and parked it next to Lucas's cubicle. "It's good to see you again," Ted said. "I was gone last week, so I hope you didn't miss me." He gave Lucas a wry smile.

"Oh?" Lucas replied. "Where did you go?"

"I was on vacation," Ted said. "My wife and I went down to Southern California to relax, soak up some sun, and spend time with an old friend I've known for a few years. Went to the beach, of course. Beautiful! I ran into a young man out there and we ended up talking over some of the same stuff you and I have been getting into. Nice fella."

"It sounds like you really enjoyed the time off," said Lucas.

"We surely did," said Ted. "So how've you been, my friend?"

"Things have been going pretty well," said Lucas. "You gave me lots to think about. I've been reflecting on the first vital question and where I put my focus. I've been noticing how often I default to that reactive way of thinking as I go through the day.

"Hey, and I also connected with someone you apparently got to know when she was managing the Customer Call Center. Do you remember—"

"Kasey!" Ted interjected. "I do remember her, very well. Soon as you mentioned the call center, I knew who you were talking about. Kasey really absorbed the three vital questions—we had some wonderful conversations."

"I could tell she learned a lot from those conversations," Lucas replied. "She and I met for coffee several weeks ago, and she walked me through some of the exercises you taught her. Since then I've been journaling about my thoughts, feelings, and actions, as well as my reactive triggers and strategies. I can't believe how often I've been reacting without even being aware of what's behind it."

"That's great!" said Ted. "I think you may be experiencing an upgrade in your internal operating system." He laughed. Then he added, "I'd like to hear some of those insights, Lucas, if you wouldn't mind."

"I'd love to." Lucas took a few minutes to read some of his journal entries to Ted. It felt good to share what he had been noticing about his reactive patterns and how—even when problems presented themselves—he had tried to stay focused on outcomes and take action from the Outcome Orientation.

"Nice job applying your insights," said Ted. "Sounds like you're not just using the approach at work, you're taking it back to the home front, too." Then he added, "Before I tell you about the second vital question, I want to tell you something important about the ideas of Victim and Creator that will get us from the first vital question to the second. That is, if you have the time."

"You bet!" said Lucas. "In fact, I stayed late today hoping we'd have another chance to talk."

"Good man." Ted continued, "I want to explain how the Problem Orientation is actually a Victim Orientation, because usually we feel victimized by the problems we're reacting to. On the other hand, the Outcome Orientation is really a Creator Orientation, from which you create outcomes and the baby steps you'll take to accomplish those outcomes. As you've already noticed, sometimes the steps you take are setbacks or mistakes. Those unexpected events make the whole process quite interesting. So there's your operating system in a nutshell. And out of this operating system you can *consciously* choose how you're going to respond to whatever comes your way."

Lucas responded, "It's been a real eye-opener to be able to notice how I'm thinking and acting throughout the day."

"That's great news, Lucas! Now that you've got a handle on the Victim and Creator Orientations, we can move on to the second of the three vital questions. You'll see that the answer to this question depends heavily on which of the two orientations, or FISBEs, you are operating in.

"The question is this: *How are you relating?* There are actually a few layers to this one, as I learned from my CEO friend. One is, *How are you relating to other people?* Another is, *How are you relating to what is going on in your life?* And the third is, *How you are relating to yourself?*

"The key here is, are you relating in ways that are going to produce or perpetuate drama, or are you relating in ways that empower yourself and others to be more resourceful, resilient, and innovative?"

The Dreaded Drama Triangle

As Ted spoke, Lucas felt he was listening in a whole new way, as though he was claiming this second vital question as his own. As the words "produce or perpetuate drama" resonated in his mind and memories, Lucas shook his head.

"Gosh, Ted, I can't tell you how much drama goes on around here. Sometimes I feel like I'm living and working in a soap opera!"

"Yes," said Ted. "Drama goes unchecked in most workplaces, I'd say. Unfortunately, it seems to be the default system that takes over many of our life situations. Drama is the natural product of an environment rooted in the Problem Orientation, which we know is also the Victim Orientation." He paused as Lucas nodded in agreement.

"Years ago," Ted continued, "a psychiatrist by the name of Stephen Karpman identified a triangle of relationship roles that make up what you might call the Dreaded Drama Triangle, or DDT. You may know that DDT is a very toxic chemical, so it's a fitting name for the toxic way these roles work their drama on one another."

Ted picked up a marker and turned to the whiteboard across from Lucas's cubicle. On it Ted drew a downward-pointing triangle. At the bottom point of the triangle he wrote *Victim.*

"The central role in the DDT is the role of Victim, Lucas. And here's a rule you can go by: anytime you find yourself complaining—whenever there is something you want or care about that you feel powerless to have, do, or be—then you know you're stuck in the Victim role," Ted explained.

"That's how I feel a lot of the time here at work," said Lucas. "And, when things get *really* bad, I feel a bit hopeless that it will ever get any better."

"I'm sure there are times when you feel victimized by things that are happening in your life, whether it's here or elsewhere," Ted said. "We all feel victimized from time to time. You can think of victimization along the lines of the old 'scale from one to ten.' Maybe at one, you're waiting in a long line at the grocery store, while on the other end of the scale, say ten, you could be in a war zone or in the midst of an earthquake, or really any situation that poses an immediate threat to your physical safety."

Lucas nodded. "Okay. I see what you mean."

"But feeling victimized is very different from *victimhood*," said Ted. "Sadly, victimhood can become a whole self-identity, a way of being in life that keeps you feeling like you have no choice, that life is just happening to you and you can't do anything to change it.

"When you ask yourself this second vital question, *How am I relating?* it's a direct challenge to that stance of victimhood. But at the same time you're acknowledging, 'Hey, this feeling of victimization is all part of the human condition. It's not who I am, it's just part of my experience.'"

Ted continued, "You don't strike me as someone who lives his life in a state of victimhood, Lucas. From what you've shared with me, it seems you have a wonderful home life. But it definitely sounds like you feel victimized by some of what's happening here at work. Is that a fair impression?"

Lucas nodded. "Yes, that's right. I'm pretty happy in life, for the most part. Though I guess you've heard me doing quite a bit of complaining about work."

"Makes sense to me." Ted raised his marker again and turned back to the whiteboard. "So anytime you—or anyone else—inhabits the Victim role, there has to be a

Persecutor. That's the second role in the Dreaded Drama Triangle." Ted wrote *Persecutor* at the upper right corner of the triangle.

"While you might think of a Persecutor as a person—like your new boss, maybe—there are other forms a Persecutor can take. It might be a health condition, such as heart disease or diabetes. The Persecutor also could be a situation such as a hurricane or earthquake, or any of the other tragic events we see on the news. Or it could just be one of those everyday annoyances like getting stuck in rush-hour traffic or being stuck in line at the grocery store, like I mentioned earlier."

Lucas sat back and considered Ted's diagram. "Okay, now I want to make sure I understand this. A Persecutor could be a person, or a condition, or a situation. I can think of a few examples. You already mentioned my boss, so that's a person. My dad was diagnosed with type 2 diabetes about ten years ago, and I remember him really feeling down about that, so I guess you could say he felt victimized by the disease. And you are absolutely right about the news! Wars, hurricanes, earthquakes, gun violence. It seems like the list of Persecutors could go on forever!"

"Those are all good examples," said Ted. "When the Persecutor is a person, often they seek to control and dominate the drama. They actually fear their own victimization, so they become aggressive. Then they can easily blame the Victim for whatever is happening.

"And whatever form the Persecutor takes, he, she, or it is

dominating the time, attention, and energy of the person in the Victim role. The Persecutor is 'the problem' that the Victim is reacting to out of fear or anxiety." Ted put down his marker. "Does that sound familiar?"

Lucas smiled. "Yes. I think you're describing the FISBE of the Problem . . . I mean, the *Victim* Orientation."

"You got it!" Ted turned back to the whiteboard. "There's one last role to complete our DDT here." As he wrote the word at the upper left corner of the triangle, he said, "And that's the Rescuer."

"Someone coming to save the day?" asked Lucas.

"Could be," responded Ted. "It could definitely be a person, but not necessarily. I'll come back to that in just a minute.

"There are three ways a Rescuer can come in and complete the DDT. One, the Victim goes looking for a Rescuer and invites them into the drama. Second, someone intervenes to either take care of or fix the Victim, or goes after the Persecutor to protect the Victim. Then the third kind of Rescuer could be someone or some situation that the Victim *hopes* will emerge to, as you say, 'save the day.'

"When a Victim goes looking for a Rescuer," Ted continued, "they may be seeking something to help them get some distance, or numb out their feelings of powerlessness or hopelessness. That something could range from zoning out and binge-watching a TV series to having an extra glass of wine, or worse. That's why I call the Rescuer the 'pain reliever.'"

"Hmm," Lucas responded. "I can see how I sometimes go home and retreat into my study to escape into social media or news sites on the internet—and sometimes, I admit, with that extra glass of wine. And when I stop to think about my situation here at the office, I can see I've been thinking of Kasey as a sort of Rescuer."

"That's a great insight, Lucas," Ted said. "If Kasey is practicing what she and I talked about—and I would bet she is—then I think you'll find she knows how to be a helpful support, without falling into the Rescuer role. See, the shadow side of the Rescuer individual is that, while their actions are usually well-intended, taking care of or fixing the Victim only reinforces the Victim's feelings of powerlessness and resentment about their victimization."

Ted went on, "And what's more, the Rescuer takes actions based on fear, too, just like the Persecutor does. The Rescuer's fear is that they will not be needed—so they seek out a Victim they can 'help.' This renews the Rescuer's sense of purpose—to fix or protect or take care of the Victim. When three individuals are involved, then all three roles—Victim, Persecutor, and Rescuer—are locked in reaction to fear, each using a different strategy to stave off that fear, of things spinning out of control.

"So, there you have it—the Dreaded Drama Triangle, better known as the toxic DDT." Ted gestured to the simple diagram he had drawn.

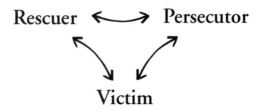

Diagram 9. The Dreaded Drama Triangle

Lucas took out his journal and drew the DDT. "I'd like to hear more, Ted. But first I want to take a few minutes to capture some notes, okay?"

"Great. I'll work my way down this corridor a little ways," Ted said, and he gave the cart a push to get it moving. "Just holler when you're ready to hear about the antidote to the toxic DDT."

"The antidote?" Lucas asked.

"Absolutely," Ted called as he headed down the aisle between the cubicles. "It's all about upgrading your orientation—your internal operating system—from the Victim Orientation to a Creator Orientation. Once you can do that, you're in for a whole new dynamic!" He waved. "I'll be happy to swing back by and share that with you when you're ready. Just holler."

Lucas scribbled a few notes from what Ted had shared about the DDT. He was looking forward to telling Kasey about what he'd just learned. He wondered how she dealt with drama in her area of the organization. And he wondered if Kasey had been able to apply any of Ted's wisdom during her time working under the same boss that Lucas worked for now.

Lucas also reflected a bit on how he and Sarah and the children could get into contentious situations at home. He could certainly see there were times when they got swept up in the DDT.

After several minutes, Lucas stood up and looked down the corridor. He could hear Ted humming, but couldn't quite see him. Then Lucas saw Ted's head pop up from several cubicles down.

"Ready when you are!" Lucas called out.

"Be there as soon as I finish dusting up over here," said Ted.

TED* (*The Empowerment Dynamic)

When Ted returned, he asked Lucas for a whiteboard eraser.

"Thanks," he said as he turned to erase the Dreaded Drama Triangle diagram.

"Wish I could say it's just this easy to erase the Victim, Persecutor, and Rescuer roles from the way we relate to one another, but I'm afraid these roles are deeply wired in human beings, and we all fall into them sometimes," said Ted.

He turned around and leaned against the whiteboard, facing Lucas. "Now that you have seen the Victim Orientation, I suspect you can see that it's our default operating system. It can run our entire lives if we let it.

But, what if I told you we could take this whole thing one step further?"

"I can't wait," said Lucas.

"There's a much more effective and enjoyable way to relate, once you start to develop a Creator Orientation," Ted continued. "The CEO I told you about—he really opened my eyes with this one. And, I have to say, I now take it rather personally."

"What do you mean?" Lucas asked.

Ted raised his marker to the whiteboard and wrote *TED* (*The Empowerment Dynamic)* at the top.

"Oh, wow!" Lucas exclaimed. "Did he name it after you?"

"Nope, I wish he had." Ted chuckled. "But I'm honored to share the same name as the triangle of roles and relationships I'm about to show you."

Lucas turned to a fresh page in his journal, picked up his pen, and smiled. "Ready when you are!"

Again Ted drew a triangle on the board, but this time it pointed upward. "Remember how I said the DDT thrives in the Victim Orientation. And how the acronym DDT is symbolic of the toxic relationships in the Dreaded Drama Triangle?"

"Absolutely."

"Well," Ted went on, pointing to the new triangle, "the roles in TED*—The Empowerment Dynamic—are the antidotes to the toxic roles of the DDT." Ted grinned. "I already gave you a hint about what the primary TED* role is, Lucas."

"You did?" Lucas squinted at the empty triangle on the whiteboard.

"Yes! Didn't I tell you I'd have a quiz for you occasionally?" Ted laughed, playfully wagging his marker.

"So, here it is: What is the antidote or—here's a big clue—the *upgrade* to the Victim Orientation?"

"Oh sure! It's a Creator Orientation," said Lucas, relieved.

Ted wrote *Creator* at the top of the triangle. "You got it. The antidote to the role of Victim is the role of *Creator*. And Creator is the central role of TED*—The Empowerment Dynamic.

"Now, being a Creator has two main characteristics. First, a Creator focuses on creating outcomes, just as we talked about earlier. The second characteristic—and this is really important—is that a Creator takes responsibility for the way they respond to whatever happens in their experience. Creators do this even when they feel victimized."

Lucas frowned. "Wait a minute. Are you saying that a Creator *chooses* a fight, flight, freeze, or appease reaction to whatever is going on? Isn't that what Victims do?"

"You're so right," Ted said. "The *choosing* is the big difference here, as well as the range of choices. There is actually a big difference between just reacting to a situation and choosing how to respond to it."

Ted put down the whiteboard marker. He reached into his back pocket, took out his wallet, and pulled out a folded piece of paper. As Ted unfolded it, Lucas could see it was well-worn around the edges.

"My CEO friend gave me this," Ted said. "Right here are three quotes from a guy named Victor Frankl, who was imprisoned in Nazi concentration camps when he was a young man—talk about being victimized! During that awful experience, Frankl had an epiphany that he credits with allowing him to survive. He explains, better than I can, why choosing our response is so much more powerful than merely reacting."

Ted handed Lucas the piece of paper. "Read it out loud, my friend."

"Sure," said Lucas. He read:

"Between stimulus and response there is a space. In that space is our power to choose our response. In our response lies our growth and our freedom."

"When we are no longer able to change a situation, we are challenged to change ourselves."

"Everything can be taken from a man but one thing: the last of the human freedoms—to choose one's attitude in any given set of circumstances, to choose one's own way."

When Lucas finished reading, he sat for a moment in silence.

Ted cleared his throat and rubbed his chin. "These words came from a man—he was a psychiatrist—who lived through one of the most horrible experiences imaginable. Yet he came to these great insights. Can you see the difference here, between reacting as a Victim, which Frankl easily could have done, versus choosing to respond as a Creator?"

"I'm almost speechless," Lucas said slowly. "This makes my challenges with my team and my new boss look like a walk in the park." He started to hand the piece of paper back to Ted.

"You keep it—it's yours now," Ted said. "I have them memorized anyway." He turned back to the board and picked up a marker. At the lower left corner of the triangle he wrote *Challenger*.

"The antidote to the DDT role of Persecutor . . . is the TED* role of *Challenger*. Challengers spark learning and growth. When something happens and you feel victimized, if you can ask 'What can I learn from this person, this condition, or this situation?' instead of reacting to it as though it's your Persecutor . . . well, then you've unlocked the secret to the Challenger role. That's what Victor Frankl did." There was a moment of silence, then Ted continued.

"Challengers call forth learning and growth. Sometimes the Challengers in your life are aware of the role they're playing. These are conscious, constructive Challengers who inspire and evoke learning. Have you ever had a boss who actively challenged you to learn and grow?"

Lucas thought for a moment. "Sure," he said. "Actually, my previous boss was good at giving me assignments that really made me stretch. In fact, he named me team lead of my group just before he was promoted. That's how I ended up reporting to my new boss. When my former boss gave me the job assignment I have now, he said it was intended to be a developmental experience—in learning to lead others. I can definitely say I'm learning a lot, even if it's not always pleasant."

Ted nodded, "Yes, exactly. Yet oftentimes the Challengers in our lives are unpleasant situations, or people . . ."

"Like my new boss," Lucas interjected.

"Like your new boss," Ted agreed. "You learn from the tough, unwanted, and unwelcome experiences as much or more than you can learn from the positive things that happen. Just one unpleasant jolt can really provoke you to learn and grow. You might call these unconscious, *deconstructive* Challengers."

Lucas frowned a little. Ted continued: "What I mean by that is, sometimes there'll be people who aren't intentionally challenging you, but you may experience them that way. When Victor Frankl had his epiphany, it gave him the amazing insights that enabled him to see his Nazi captors as Challengers, rather than as Persecutors. And he did it by 'deconstructing' the situation to discover what he could learn from it."

Ted went on, "Also, when you experience something like an illness or an accident, you can't really say those circumstances or situations are conscious in the human sense. So you may have to dig to find the lessons hidden in them. You mentioned that your dad had diabetes. I'll bet he learned a lot from that situation."

Lucas responded, "As a matter of fact, he did. Dad shared with me some of the lessons he learned about the importance of diet and exercise and how the body processes sugar, that sort of thing. So, yes, I can say he learned from diabetes as a Challenger."

"There you go," said Ted. "The bottom line is that Challengers call out our potential for learning and growth. And, when you take on the role of a Creator, you can look at virtually any experience as an opportunity to learn."

On the whiteboard Ted wrote the word *Coach* under the lower right corner of the TED* triangle and said: The antidote to the role of Rescuer in the DDT is the role of **Coach** in TED*.

"A Coach supports a Creator," said Ted, "by asking questions that help clarify that Creator's intended outcomes or help the Creator to see their current reality more clearly. Coaches also help Creators understand what they're learning and support them in deciding what actions they'll take.

"In the Dreaded Drama Triangle, a Rescuer may be well-intentioned, but they actually end up reinforcing the Victim's sense of powerlessness. In The Empowerment Dynamic, a Coach respects the person or group they are supporting by seeing them as ultimately creative and resourceful. A true Coach will never try to take away a Creator's power to choose their own responses and actions. Unlike a Rescuer, a Coach knows how to help while leaving that power with the Creator, where it belongs."

Lucas nodded as he finished copying the TED* triangle into his journal. "I know some people, like our friend Kasey, work with an executive coach when they're engaged in executive leadership development."

"That's true—and that is a professional coach," said

Ted. "But the role of Coach we're talking about in TED*
here, that doesn't have to be a trained professional. Not at
all. You can act as a Coach right now in your leadership
role with your team. You can be a Coach with your friends
and family members. Believe it or not, you can even be a
Coach with your boss."

"You're kidding!" Lucas laughed.

"Anytime you're asking questions to clarify outcomes,
to help others and yourself think through things, you're
being a Coach. It's an important part of being a leader,"
said Ted.

"Hmm." Lucas mused. "I'll have to sit with that idea
for a while. It's pretty hard to imagine being a Coach with
my boss."

Ted chuckled. He placed the cap on the marker and set
it down in the tray of the whiteboard.

"One more thing," Ted said, "and then it's back to work
for me.

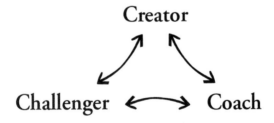

Creator

Challenger ⟷ **Coach**

Diagram 10. TED*
(*The Empowerment Dynamic)

"Just as all three roles in the DDT are Victim-oriented . . . in TED*, the roles of Creator, Challenger, and Coach are Creator-oriented. And you can shift in and out of these three roles as you go about co-creating outcomes and choosing responses to any challenges you have with others." Ted pointed to the new triangle on the board.

Lucas looked down at the TED* triangle in his journal, then flipped back to the previous page, where he had drawn the DDT. As Ted returned to his cart, Lucas said, "I just noticed the TED* triangle is pointing upward while the DDT points downward. Is there a reason for that?"

"Nothing gets past you, does it?" Ted laughed. "There's definitely a reason for that! The DDT points down to show that this triangle of relationships is unstable—it symbolizes the 'downer' or negative energy between the three roles.

"On the other hand, the TED* triangle sits on a solid base and points upward, quite optimistically. It symbolizes how, as a Creator, you're focused on continuing to grow and develop, and to create positive outcomes."

"I like that." said Lucas. "The upward energy of being a Creator and learning to co-create with others as a Challenger and Coach—that's what I want. Oh, and I'm having coffee with Kasey again in a couple of days. I'm looking forward to talking with her about the DDT and your namesake—TED*."

As he began rolling the cart away, Ted grinned. "You can learn a lot from that Kasey. Give her my regards, my friend."

CHAPTER SIX

Seeing Differently

Lucas and Sarah were having a date night: dinner and a movie. At dinner, Lucas was bursting with all he had learned from Ted.

"And I think Kasey, our neighbor, can help me use this stuff with my boss, too," he said. "She knows what he's like, and she has more practice with this stuff than I do. Ted even said I could potentially be a Coach to my boss."

Sarah was intrigued. "Wow, that sounds amazingly encouraging. I know what a strain it's been for you trying to work with that guy. It would be great if this approach makes a difference there."

Lucas laughed. "I'm definitely going to give it my best effort!"

The two talked about the Dreaded Drama Triangle and The Empowerment Dynamic for so long that they decided to scratch the movie and head to a quiet bistro for a nightcap. There, Sarah and Lucas talked about ways they saw the DDT at work sometimes in their marriage— especially when there were issues with the children. They committed to each other to call a time-out whenever they noticed either of them falling into a Victim, Persecutor, or Rescuer role. Lucas and Sarah agreed that they wanted to raise their kids as Creators. They knew this would mean practicing the TED* approach with their children on a regular basis, and they were excited to think of the ways this could strengthen their relationships—with each other and as a family.

They held hands on the way to the car, and Sarah said, "This was one of our best dates in a long time."

"Yeah." Lucas smiled. "I really like sharing this stuff with you. It's like we're starting something new together. It feels great."

The next morning, Lucas met Kasey at the Java Junction, the other coffee shop in their building, which housed the headquarters of the financial services behemoth they worked in. Lucas shared with Kasey some of his conversation with Sarah and how it had seemed to reenergize their relationship.

"I can definitely relate to that," Kasey said. "When I was learning about the 3 Vital Questions from Ted, I'd go home and share what I was learning with my husband, Frank. It really made a difference in our communication with each other, and with our kids—once we got the hang of it. I was happier at home *and* I started feeling a lot happier at work.

"Of course, I've also found that even though the ideas are simple, they're not always easy to apply."

Lucas took a sip of his latte and nodded. "I can imagine that's true. It's just that I'm so excited about everything I'm learning here. I can see the real possibility of thinking differently and relating to people differently. Once you learn about the DDT, you start seeing it everywhere—in movies and TV, advertising, politics—you name it."

"I couldn't agree more," Kasey said. "The more I started to notice the DDT here at work, the more I came to realize that the Victim role isn't limited to individuals. Groups of people can feel victimized all together!

"For instance," she said, "it could be a team feeling victimized by changes or assignments they've been given. I've seen whole departments feeling victimized by other departments in the organization. Even an entire organization can feel victimized—by competitors or regulations or changes in the marketplace. In every case, they're seeing the problem as a Persecutor, which causes them to react, which keeps them stuck in the Victim Orientation and the DDT."

"I see what you mean," Lucas said. "I hadn't thought about that, but it makes a lot of sense. I think my whole team has been reacting like Victims to our new boss— and it's so easy to see him as a Persecutor. Some of the changes he's initiated, and the sharp style of his feedback on reports, can really get us down at times."

Kasey blew on her hot coffee to cool it a bit. "Something you might consider, Lucas, is that it isn't your boss's intent to be a Persecutor at all. In his own way, he might think he's actually being more of a Rescuer."

"How do you mean?" Lucas asked. He was stunned, and it probably showed.

"Don't get me wrong," said Kasey. "I'm not defending him or how he goes about doing what he does." She paused.

"Lucas, I'm going to share an insight I had several months ago about my own leadership style. Realizing this has given me a lot more compassion for myself, and for others who work in leadership roles. And I think you know that my bias is to believe that everyone has a leadership role, even if it's only expressed in the way they relate to their co-workers.

"I appreciate your willingness to share your insights," said Lucas, adding, "And I completely agree that we're all practicing leadership, in one way or another."

"I thought so," said Kasey with a smile. "I was fortunate to go through a really good executive leadership development program. One of the last experiences I had in that program was receiving feedback from others about their perceptions of me as a leader. We were using a powerful multi-rater feedback system called the Leadership Circle Profile. I got feedback from my boss—not *your* current boss, but *my* current boss. I also received feedback from my peers, my direct reports, and a few other people I'd worked with on different projects during the two years I was in the program.

"I had always prided myself on my people skills. I felt confident that I was a pretty good leader during my rotation of assignments over that two-year period. Overall, I'm glad to say, the feedback was pretty good and did confirm a lot of that."

"I can't say I'm surprised," said Lucas.

"But that's not really what I wanted to share," Kasey continued. "That's only the context for what really got my attention.

"One of the unique aspects of the feedback was that I learned about the perceptions other people form around what the Leadership Circle Profile calls our *Reactive Tendencies*, or reactive strategies. These strategies are usually formed very early in life. They're how people—all of us— try to gain a sense of worth and identity and to control the uncontrollable situations we find ourselves in as children. We then take those childhood ways of reacting into our adult lives and, of course, into our ways of leading as well.

"There are three Reactive Tendencies that the Leadership Circle Profile provides feedback on. They're called *Controlling, Protecting,* and *Complying.* Everyone learns aspects of all three of these styles, but people tend to develop one or two of these as their main way of reacting.

"And here's the kicker: there's a close relationship between those Reactive Tendencies and the roles in the Dreaded Drama Triangle.

"All three of these strategies—to control, protect, or comply—are attempts to avoid feeling victimized by circumstances. Those who tend to be more *controlling* are often perceived as Persecutors, especially when their attempts to control are combined with some protective behaviors. Leaders who are perceived as more *compliant* often show up as Rescuers—and that's the tendency I recognized in myself."

Kasey stopped for a moment. "Is this making sense so far?" she asked.

"Sort of," said Lucas. "I think I can see how a controlling person shows up as a Persecutor, but I'm not really clear on what you mean by complying being related to being a Rescuer."

"Well," said Kasey, "here's what I realized when I saw that people perceived me as being compliant at times. I can sometimes be a people-pleaser. I can 'go along to get along,' as the saying goes. My profile confirmed that I have strong people and relationship skills, but sometimes I'd let people off the hook or avoid stepping up to some of the difficult conversations I really should have been having. In the language of The Empowerment Dynamic, I wasn't being a conscious Challenger of others. Sometimes I'd take care of things for people—things that were really their responsibility—because I didn't want to make waves."

Lucas leaned back in his seat and sighed. "Ouch. I can relate to that. Just the other day, I edited one of my teammates' reports. I figured it would be easier to do it myself than to point out to him what needed to be changed."

Kasey smiled. "Now can you see how that's being a Rescuer?"

"I do now," said Lucas.

Kasey continued, "And there is another form of Rescuing that I realized I sometimes fell into. It's what my coach called being a 'hero manager.' I would step in and either fix someone's work, or try to fix the person themselves—in a sense, I wanted to save the day. Even controlling types can fall into this category of Rescuer. They'll make decisions that others could or should make, or tell people what to do and insist it be done that way. They feel like they should have all the answers. And if they don't have answers, they pretend to, because it's easier than admitting they don't know.

"This is what I wonder about when it comes to your new boss," Kasey said. "There may be times when he's actually trying to save the day, but his way of going about it comes across as persecution. Again, I'm just wondering. What do you think?"

"Gosh, I have to admit it never occurred to me that he might be trying to be a Rescuer," Lucas said. He leaned his elbow on the table and took another swig of his latte. "I thought I had him figured out, but I can see I'm going to have to pay more attention to the possible reasons behind his way of doing things." One of many things he was going to have to pay more attention to.

"So, I'm curious, Kasey," Lucas said. "What difference has all that feedback made in the way you approach your leadership role now?"

"I received my leadership-style feedback several months after I learned about the DDT and TED* from our friend Ted," said Kasey. "At first I got down on myself for the ways I was unwittingly acting as a Rescuer. I also came to see how there might be times that my attempts to rescue could actually be perceived by others as persecution. That was really tough.

"For instance, I kept thinking about this one project, where I'd led a team of peers—we were tasked with redesigning the new-employee orientation process. It was such an exciting new development for our division of the company, and all of us were jazzed about being a part of it. But whenever there was a disagreement in a meeting, I'd try to move things along by suggesting a solution or saying that we'd decide the issue later. Also, there was one team member who seemed to delight in being the naysayer, always saying why this or that wouldn't work. It was really slowing us down, and I was worried we weren't going to make the project deadline. So when there were disagreements in meetings, I began to email people afterward. I'd thank them for their ideas and then suggest my own solution. I hoped that would smooth things over and get us back on track.

"After a while, though, the energy of the team seemed to just flatten out completely. It was awful. Instead of the initial enthusiasm we had all shared, I felt like I was trying to start a car in a subzero snowstorm—there just was no energy to start the engine, and I couldn't clearly see where I wanted us to go, either." Kasey sighed.

"Not only did we not make our deadline, but the project was reassigned to another team. I felt my team members blamed me for that." She took a sip of coffee, frowning.

"Anyway, after getting feedback on my leadership style and my Reactive Tendencies, I saw what it was I'd been doing on that project that had, in effect, sabotaged it. I was both fleeing and appeasing, basically, by not working through the issues in the meetings, and then trying to provide all the answers to the disagreements myself. It was terribly humbling—and a huge learning experience.

"So, after I got over my wounded pride, I shifted my

focus toward cultivating a style of leading as a Creator, Challenger, and Coach. One of the things I've really been working on since then is holding those on my team responsible and accountable for their jobs and the areas they lead. It's a much more balanced way to work. And I can still be supportive of them as a Challenger and a Coach."

Kasey's phone buzzed. "I have to check this," she said apologetically as she picked it up. Then: "Sorry, Lucas, but I just got a text about some questions my boss has, so I really need to go. I hope our conversation has been helpful to you. It's been a nice refresher for me."

"You have no idea," Lucas said. He took the last sip of his latte as he stood up. "You've given me a lot to think about in my own little leadership role. Talking with you has been really helpful, and I can't thank you enough."

As they gathered up their things and dropped their cups in the recycling bin, Kasey asked, "When do you think you'll see Ted again?"

"I'm not sure. It won't be tonight, though," said Lucas. "Sarah and I have a school open house to go to, so I'll be leaving right at the end of the day. But I hope to stay late in a couple of days and see Ted then."

"Well, when you do see Ted again," said Kasey, "ask him if he'll share with you how to make shifts happen."

"How to make shifts happen?" said Lucas.

Kasey smiled as she reached for the door. "Yes, how to make shifts happen—from the DDT to the TED* roles. Oh, and tell him I said hello!"

CHAPTER SEVEN

Making Shifts Happen

As Lucas was driving to work the next morning, he found himself replaying the experience that he and Sarah had had at the school open house. Their daughter Emily's third-grade teacher had enthused at length about her and, like any parent would, they had beamed with pride. But their next conference, with Carson's first-grade teacher, had gone quite differently. Lucas had felt his anxiety rising as the teacher explained that their son seemed to be having attention issues, that he was a bit "too social" and sometimes disrupted class.

On the way home, he and Sarah had talked about how to support their little boy in becoming more attentive and not getting into trouble at school. They talked about what they were going to say to Carson in the morning—by the time they got home, the babysitter would already have him in bed.

Sarah was the one to point out that, in fact, they were reacting to what the teacher had said and seeing their son as a problem to solve.

"Boy, you got that right!" Lucas said, amazed by his wife's insight. "It's great to see how you're applying what Ted has been sharing with me."

Sarah had always been a quick study, with a keen sense of intuition about the kids, but this approach was new for both of them. Together they realized that their anxiety had them caught in a Victim Orientation. They agreed they wanted to treat Carson as a Creator—even though he was only six years old. At that, they both went silent for a moment. It was a little scary, but it also felt like they were standing at the threshold of some great new possibilities as parents.

Lucas asked, "Okay, so what outcome do we want here? And how can the two of us be loving Challengers and maybe even Coaches for Carson?" They spent the rest of the ride home brainstorming. They would talk with Carson before school the next morning.

Sarah sat next to Carson at the breakfast counter to tell him that they'd talked to his teacher and heard that he seemed to be having a tough time paying attention and had been talking a lot with other kids during class.

As he poured coffee into a travel mug for his ride to work, Lucas said, "I was a little surprised, Carson, because I've seen you be so focused at other times, like when you're playing T-ball. I know you can pay attention when it's something you care about."

Carson looked down at his bowl of cereal. He said, "I do care about school. One day Ms. Pease brought her two hamsters to class. I got to feed them pieces of carrot while she told us all about them. Did you know a hamster can hold almost two whole meals in his cheeks before he really eats it? I saw one do it with the carrots—his cheeks got gigantic!"

Sarah patted Carson on the back. "It sounds like that was a really special day, honey. I love seeing you so excited about school." Then she stepped right into the TED* Coach role and asked, "Sometimes, though, it sounds like you get so excited that you might be disturbing the class. What else could you do with all that excitement? Is there another time or place to burn off your excited energy?"

"I don't know," Carson said. "My excited energy just jumps out sometimes."

Lucas and Sarah smiled—and stifled the temptation to jump in and make suggestions with their own excited energy. Carson thought for a long minute.

"Maybe on the playground or in gym class," he said, nodding as if imagining it. "I'll try." Their son was working on his own solution!

Lucas busied himself by buttering a piece of toast. "Carson, do you think you might be talking to your friends a little too much during class?"

"Jay sits right behind me and always teases me and whispers stuff to me, so it's not my fault. What am I supposed to do when he cracks me up all the time? If I laugh or say something back, I get in trouble with the teacher. It's not fair."

"What could you do to not react to Jay?" Lucas asked.

"I don't know!" Carson blurted in frustration. "He's my friend, but I wish I didn't sit so close to him." He took a long drink of his juice, then looked up at his mom with teary eyes. "Do you think the teacher would let me move to another seat?"

Sarah smiled and gave him a high five. "I think that would be great, sweetie. When I take you to school today, do you think you could ask your teacher if it's possible to move to another place in the classroom?"

Carson thought it over, then asked, "Can you go in with me when I ask her?"

"I'll be with you for support, buddy," Sarah said as she rubbed his head.

Carson smiled back with a big, hearty nod. "Good! I can do that."

Their conversation with Carson had taken all of twenty minutes.

Shifting Roles

As Lucas pulled into the parking garage at work, he felt a sense of satisfaction that he and Sarah had put into practice what they were learning. They had both been nothing short of amazed at how smoothly their talk with Carson had gone.

Then, as Lucas remembered that the second half of his morning would include a team meeting with his peers and his new boss, his mood turned glum. He made his way to the elevator, mentally preparing for the worst.

"Wait a minute," he said to himself as he waited for the doors to open. "What if I stopped reacting to my boss as a problem and practiced some of what Kasey said yesterday? He might be trying to be a Rescuer, after all. I'm going to try to listen differently in the meeting today and see if that changes anything."

The morning started with a team huddle of his data analysts, as it did every Monday, Wednesday, and Friday when they met to talk about what was on their plates for the next couple of days. As they were wrapping up, Lucas asked one of his team members, Tim, to come by and see him about the analysis report Lucas had received the night before.

In the past, Lucas would have put on his Rescuer hat and edited that report. This time, he was determined to take a lesson from Kasey's experience and leave space for his teammate to fulfill his own responsibility without Lucas stepping in to "save the day."

Lucas sat down with Tim and asked several questions about the report—including what suggestions Tim would make to management about what the analysis indicated. Not surprisingly, Tim had a few good ideas about how to use the data to improve their company's service to the customer. That was their prime objective, after all.

Lucas handed Tim a hard copy of the report. "I know you had a deadline to get this to me by last night, and I appreciate you getting it to me on time. But you can make this report even more useful to the people who rely on us to provide both information and suggestions. So I want you to look over the report and see what edits you can make if you put yourself in the shoes of the folks we'll be sending it to. Also, please add a short section with your suggested actions based on the data. Can you do that and have it back to me by the end of the day?"

Tim looked a little stunned. "Uh, sure . . . okay. I guess

before, you usually used to add suggestions after I gave you my reports, so I thought all you wanted was the data. I do have some ideas about what they should do with it, though, so I can definitely add that."

Lucas nodded. "You're right about the way I used to handle your reports, but now I'd like you to add your thinking, because I can tell from our conversations that you have good instincts. Let's meet at four-thirty, and we can look at your report together. Then if I have anything to add to your suggestions, we can talk that through."

"Sounds good. Thanks for asking for my input."

Wow, his teammate had actually thanked him! Lucas had dreaded giving this feedback, fearing the guy might resent having to do more work. Instead, Lucas realized, he had just succeeded in becoming a Challenger to his associate. Not only that, but by not taking over the data report and doing the work himself, Lucas had stopped assuming the role of Rescuer.

Shifting Focus

And now it was time for Lucas's monthly meeting with his boss and fellow team leads and supervisors. Together, everyone in the meeting held responsibility for the organization's customer service data analytics.

As Lucas entered the room, he readily saw that he wasn't the only one feeling uneasy. Half a dozen men and women were taking their places around the conference room table in silence. Those already seated were staring at their smartphones. Maybe they had messages they needed to respond to, but Lucas thought there was a nervous feeling in the room, with so many people avoiding eye contact.

At precisely the time the meeting was scheduled to begin, Lucas's boss hurried into the room and took his place at the head of the table. "Okay, people," he said curtly, "let's get started." He looked down the table. "The main agenda item I have for our meeting today has to do with the number of reports that get returned by our internal customers asking for more information or rework." He singled out the man sitting to Lucas's right and said, "Mark, your return rate last month was over 25 percent, and that is downright unacceptable."

Mark shifted in his seat, turned beet-red, and mumbled, "I'm sorry. I'm down two people on my team and everyone is overworked."

"That doesn't cut it," their boss replied. "No results plus a good excuse still equals no results! And that goes for everyone around the table. Things have got to change. From now on, I want every report that comes back for more info or rework to be shared with me."

Lucas felt his anxiety start to rise and noticed, once again, how he saw his boss as a Persecutor who made those around him feel like Victims. But this time Lucas tried to respond differently. He paused, took a deep breath, and started to wonder what might be behind his boss's tirade.

Their boss continued, "I've also noticed in the months I've been here that each group seems to have its own way of formatting the reports. If I were one of our customers, I wouldn't know what to expect from the next report I was about to receive."

Lucas decided to take a risk. Heart pounding, he raised his hand. When his boss stopped and looked at him, Lucas said, "Can I ask a question?"

"Go ahead," his boss said.

Lucas stammered a little, but went for it. "Can you help me understand, uh, what outcomes you want for the reports we produce? I mean, how can we improve what we deliver?"

The boss put down his pen and leaned into the table. "Fair question, Lucas. I've been thinking about that quite a lot. I want you all to produce reports that are useful to our clients. They deserve to get information that helps them make informed decisions and in a format that is easy to read and understand."

"And I heard you say that one problem seems to be that our teams produce reports in different formats," said Lucas.

"That's right, there's a lot of inconsistency."

Lucas, feeling a little emboldened, said, "I would be willing to work with someone to suggest a consistent format for reports. Just this morning, while working with one of my folks, it occurred to me to start adding suggestions for our clients in our reports, in addition to the good data and analysis we're already including. That's one component I'd want to add."

His boss looked around the room and asked, "Would anyone be willing to work with Lucas on a project like this?"

A couple hands went up. The woman across from Lucas asked, "Would it be possible to convene a focus group of some kind—maybe a cross-section of our client base—to get their input on what they're looking for, along with some ideas for formatting reports?"

The boss scratched his chin and said, "Tell you what, I'll give you all thirty days to come back to me with recommendations. I'm glad to see you step forward like this. I thought I was going to have to bring the solutions to the returns and inconsistency I've been seeing. Let's see what you come up with."

Their boss actually smiled a little, and the energy in the room seemed to shift.

Lucas looked around at the faces of his colleagues. They were relaxed, expectant. "This must be the impact of shifting from focusing on problems to focusing on outcomes," he thought. "Maybe this stuff can really work!"

Shifting to Possibility

At four-thirty, Lucas met with his teammate Tim as promised. Tim's updated analysis report and suggestions were excellent. Lucas only needed to add one suggestion, and then the two of them edited and finalized the report together on Lucas's laptop. They hit Send, and the report was on its way to the manager who had requested it. Tim, author of the report, left with a smile and said, "Thanks for asking for my input on the recommendations for the client. That was actually fun."

After Tim left, Lucas sat reflecting on the events of the day: Sarah's and his talk with Carson, the team meeting with his boss, and the way he had upgraded his expectations of his teammate only moments ago.

Down at the end of the corridor, the door opened, and Lucas heard the upbeat sound of a now-familiar song. As Ted approached, humming as he cleaned, Lucas took out his journal and began jotting down a few thoughts about his day.

When Ted was only a few cubicles away, Lucas stood up and said, "Hello, my friend. Good to see you!"

"Good to be seen, young man," said Ted. "You hanging around to visit a little while, or do you need to get home to that nice family of yours?"

"Here to hang around for a little while, if you have a moment or two," said Lucas. "I've had an interesting twenty-four hours."

"Do tell," said Ted. He deposited his feather duster and rag in a small bin attached to the cleaning cart.

Lucas shared his synopsis of the interactions of the day, starting at home and ending here at the office.

"Sounds like you've been doing good work, Lucas," Ted said, leaning against the whiteboard.

"Thanks," Lucas said. He felt pleased and, he had to admit, a little proud. "Oh, by the way, I had coffee with Kasey again yesterday. She says hello and told me to ask you about how to make shifts happen, from the Dreaded Drama Triangle to The Empowerment Dynamic roles."

"Sounds to me like that's what you've been doing

all day, my friend!" Ted grinned. "I'm happy to share a few additional thoughts. But I have to say, in all three of the situations you just described, I think you already made shifts happen, from the problem-focused Victim Orientation to an outcome-focused Creator Orientation. I'll explain what I mean.

"With your young son, you and your wife shifted to focusing on co-creating with him an outcome for how he acts when he's at school. Instead of treating him like a Victim, you two treated him as a Creator. And then in that meeting with your team member, you could have been a Rescuer, but instead you were a Challenger, by focusing on outcomes for his report and encouraging his growth and learning.

"And hey, I liked hearing about the meeting with your boss. That one really blows me away! It seems like you actually became a Coach in that situation, by asking him what kind of outcomes he had in mind, and then, as a Creator, you volunteered to co-create something with your colleagues that will help him accomplish those outcomes."

Lucas beamed. "I was just writing about some of that in my journal," he said. "I really do think I made some shifts. In all three situations I paused and made some conscious choices to change the way I was relating to people."

"And that is how shifts happen, my friend!" Ted clapped his hands. "Doesn't it feel great?"

"It sure does," said Lucas. "I can see all kinds of possibilities opening up, just from the shifts I made today."

Internal Shifts and External Shifts

"In some ways," Ted said, "I could just say, 'Keep on doing what you're doing. Keep on making those shifts happen.' You're off to a great start. But maybe it will help if I tell you about the different kinds of shifts that can take place when you move from the DDT roles to the TED* roles. Would that be helpful?"

"You bet!" said Lucas, picking up his journal and pen.

"First thing to know," said Ted, "is that shifts can happen either internally or externally."

"How do you mean?" asked Lucas.

"The internal shift happens when you change the way you think and respond to the stuff going on around you—that's an inside-out shift. First you shift to seeing yourself as a Creator. Then, once you really see yourself that way, you begin to realize all people are Creators.

"That's what happened when you and Sarah changed your focus so that instead of reacting to Carson as a problem, you chose to see him as a Creator and to work together toward an outcome. You made an *internal* shift in your perception of Carson—seeing him not as *Victim* but as *Creator*—and it changed the way you spoke with your son. That internal shift will then have an impact on the second kind of shift—the external shift.

"The *external* shift has to do with the way you relate to others and to whatever's going on around you. Once you make the internal shift, then just naturally you're going to show up differently to those around you.

"Both of your examples from here at work—when you

encouraged your team member and when you shifted things in the group meeting with your boss—are external shifts. In both situations, those folks probably saw you as a Creator, Challenger, *and* Coach, if you think about it."

"Hmm. I guess you're right," Lucas said.

"If you want to get more consistent about showing up in these TED* roles, then first and foremost, be sure to make that internal shift to seeing yourself as a Creator . . . by taking responsibility for the outcomes you focus on and the choices you make. Now, would you like to take a deeper look at how to shift roles?" Ted asked.

"Sure!" said Lucas.

CHAPTER EIGHT

Discovering the Choice Point

"The core shift takes you from Victim to Creator," Ted said. "When you choose to adopt a Creator Orientation and shift your focus from problems to outcomes—focusing on what you *do* want instead of what you *don't* want—then you're making *the* fundamental internal shift. You're upgrading your human operating system.

"And that carries you over into the external shift. You interact differently with others. When this happens, you'll also find yourself interacting with external circumstances differently, because now you're aware that you have a choice about how you respond to whatever happens around you. That's what you did in the group meeting with your boss. You first made the internal shift from being a Victim in his presence to stepping into your Creator self. That changed the way you interacted with him in the meeting, in ways that your boss and others responded to."

Lucas interjected, "But how do I get someone else who's playing the Victim to make the shift. How can I get them to take up the role of Creator?"

Ted laid his hand on Lucas's shoulder, looked him straight in the eye, and said, "You can't."

"Wait. What?" Lucas stammered.

"Here's the reality, Lucas," Ted said, leaning against the whiteboard. "You can't *make* someone shift. If you really see that everyone is a Creator in their own right—whether or not they know it or act like it—then you have to accept that they hold the power to make their own choice. You still have the choice to see them as a Creator at heart, though, even if they're choosing to play the Victim.

"The best thing you can do is to keep on being a Creator in what *you* do and say. You can encourage someone else to make the shift, maybe give them a cheerful nudge. But you definitely can't make them change."

Lucas responded, "But what if I've shared the DDT and TED* roles with them? Shouldn't I be able to just point out when they're being a Victim?"

"Think about it," Ted responded. "If I called you a Victim, how would you feel?"

Lucas frowned a little. He leaned back in his chair, closed his eyes, and took in the question. "Hmm," he said. "I think I'd feel victimized."

"Yes. You'd probably feel defensive at being labeled as a Victim, and you'd see me as a Persecutor. Then you'd jump right into reacting from inside the DDT. The dreaded drama would begin!"

"Isn't there anything I can do to help someone make that shift?" asked Lucas.

The Commitment Behind the Complaint

Ted smiled. "Yes, there are ways you can help, Lucas, but none of them are foolproof. As I've applied this shift myself, I've learned a harsh reality, and that is that you can't argue with someone else's feelings of victimization." He sighed, then added, "On second thought, you can *argue* with them, but you can't talk them out of it.

"Do you remember, from when we talked about the Victim role earlier, that when someone is feeling victimized, they have some dream or desire that they see as being denied to them?"

"Yes," Lucas replied. "There's something they care about, and in some way or another, they feel powerless or hopeless about it."

"That, my friend, gives you a clue about how you might encourage them to shift. There's a saying I heard once: 'Behind every complaint lies a commitment.' Let me ask you this: do you ever complain about something you don't care about?"

"No, I guess not," said Lucas. "I mean, why would I complain if I didn't care?"

"Exactly!" Ted responded. "If someone's acting like a Victim, then right behind their feelings of victimization, you'll find something they care about.

"So here's what you can try if you want to help someone shift. First and foremost, let them know you hear their anger or frustration or whatever their inner state is. Then subtly invite them to shift. After they see that you understand how they feel, you might say something like, 'I can tell you really care about . . .' whatever it is you think lies behind their victimization.

"You kind of did that today with your boss, even if you didn't mention his inner state. He was complaining about what he didn't want—you figured out what he did want in the reports that come from his department. Then you shifted the focus to what he cared about."

"Yeah, I guess I did do that." Lucas smiled.

"There are just a couple more things to keep in mind about this Victim-to-Creator shift," said Ted. "First is that you go from feeling hopeless or powerless—as a Victim—to being energized about the creative possibilities—as a Creator. The other is that you shift from reacting to choosing. Creators always know they have the power to choose."

Shifting From Persecutor to Challenger

Lucas briefly glanced at his watch. Ted said, "Let's move on to the second major shift from DDT to TED* roles—the Persecutor-to-Challenger shift.

"We've already talked about the internal shift, about choosing your response to whatever happens in your life. Whenever someone or something shows up in your experience—something that, before, you'd have reacted to as if it were a Persecutor in the DDT—you now have the opportunity to pause and reflect on what you might learn from the experience. In other words, you experience that person or situation as a Challenger urging you to learn something.

"And the key to helping other people see *you* as a conscious, constructive Challenger in your relationships," Ted went on, "is to know what your *intention* is."

Lucas was puzzled. "What do you mean by my intention, exactly?"

"Before you challenge someone, it's important to ask yourself if your intention is to make yourself look good, or to encourage learning and growth," Ted answered. "If your intention is to be right, to show how smart you are, to win or one-up someone, then your intention is only to look good—and that just about guarantees you'll be seen as a Persecutor.

"But a Challenger is always constructive, coming from an intention to foster learning. A Challenger's focus is on enhancing someone's capabilities. A Challenger is motivated by respect and care. A Challenger's actions might be what you'd call tough love, or at other times, a gentle nudge and a bit of direction."

"Like I did with my guy this morning when I asked him to do more work on his analysis report?" Lucas asked.

"Exactly," Ted said. "You were doing that to enhance his learning and growth, not as a one-up or a put-down. Challengers build others up, while Persecutors only criticize, which makes others feel small or less-than.

"The truth is, you can't control how someone else responds to your challenge. Either way, they could still react to you as a Persecutor. But if your intention is clearly positive and meant to enhance their learning, chances are greater that they'll rise to the occasion to learn.

"Oh, and one last point about this shift," Ted added. "It means you're moving from controlling—which is what a Persecutor is trying to do—to compassion."

"Compassion?" said Lucas.

"Yes, compassion. Because learning and growth isn't always fun and easy," said Ted. "But compassion doesn't mean all soft words and gentleness either. Remember, one of the qualities of a Challenger is being a truth teller, so it naturally means treating the other person as a Creator in their own right . . ."

"Whether they know it or not or act like it or not," Lucas filled in.

"You got it!" Ted smiled. "As a Creator, the person you're challenging has the power to choose what they do, just as much as you do. But even as you hold them responsible and accountable for the consequences of the choices they make—you can do that with compassion for their learning process."

Shifting From Rescuer to Coach

"Got time for one more?" Ted asked.

"Sure, let's go for it," said Lucas.

"The internal shift for a Rescuer is often the most difficult."

"Why is that?"

"Because Rescuers are so focused on taking care of others that they don't take time to focus on their own self-care," said Ted. "They find it very difficult to ask for support from others. Rescuers usually think they should do it all by themselves."

Lucas shook his head. "Boy, I can really relate to that one."

"So, the internal shift—that is, in how a Rescuer relates to their own experience—comes from knowing when to ask others for support," Ted said. "This isn't a sign of weakness or of playing the role of Victim. It's the act of a Creator to ask someone for help or coaching. You're not asking them to be your Rescuer—just to be a support and a buddy when you feel stuck or whatever.

"The key to shifting from a Rescuer to a Coach for others is, first and foremost, to see the people you coach as basically capable and resourceful. Along with that, a Coach recognizes that everyone holds the responsibility for the choices they make."

Lucas said, "That sounds like the same thing you said about the Challenger."

"It's pretty similar," Ted agreed. "Both a Challenger and a Coach see the other person as a Creator in their own right. A Coach's basic toolkit is asking questions that support others to clarify, and then to commit to action."

"Clarify what?" said Lucas.

"There are three main ways to get clarity. One is to clarify the outcome you want to create, the second is to clearly recognize and then speak the truth about your current reality, and the third way is to get clear about the actions, or baby steps, you're going to take.

"The next time we talk, Lucas, I can share a little more

about how all this works. But for now, it's enough to know this: the shift from Rescuer to Coach means letting go of trying to fix someone and instead moving toward supporting their empowerment. It also means that, instead of telling someone what to do or doing it for them, you begin asking questions.

"Coaches practice the mantra 'Ask first, tell second.'"

The Choice Point

Ted turned to the whiteboard, picked up a marker, and said, "One last thing before you go, and then I'll get back to my rounds."

He drew a large asterisk. At the end of each line he wrote the name of a TED* role opposite its DDT counterpart. In the center of the asterisk, Ted drew a small circle with an arrow pointing to it. He labeled the arrow: *Choice Point.*

"As you go through your day, Lucas, you have lots of opportunities to either react to people and situations from the DDT roles of Victim, Persecutor, and Rescuer . . . or, you can respond to those people or experiences from the point of view of a Creator, Challenger, or Coach. In every situation, you'll find yourself at the intersection of all these roles. You'll be standing right here." Ted placed his marker in the center of the circle. "At the choice point."

He looked at Lucas. "From here you can shift into any of the TED* roles. You don't always have to go to the exact opposite of the DDT role. For example, in your work with your team member today—instead of reacting as a Rescuer, you shifted into the Challenger role, like we talked about."

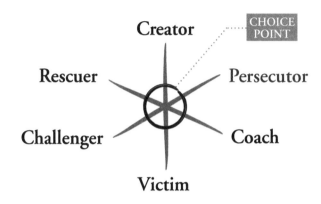

Diagram 11. The Choice Point

Ted put the cap back on the marker. "And that's how shifts happen, my friend. Any other questions before I go?"

"My mind is swimming with questions." Lucas stood up, closed his laptop, and slipped it into his backpack. "But they'll have to wait. I want to get home and share this new stuff with Sarah. I can't wait to tell her about my amazing day."

"And I need to get back to my rounds, maintaining an environment where you can do your best work—as a Creator, Challenger, and Coach." Ted chuckled as he aimed his cart back down the corridor.

"Thanks, Ted. See you later." Lucas shouldered his backpack and headed for the elevator.

As he sat behind the wheel ready for the drive home, Lucas decided to leave a voicemail for Kasey: "Hung out with Ted again tonight. Lots to share. Time for coffee in a day or two?"

CHAPTER NINE

Lessons From Experience

That night, just before dinner, Lucas and Sarah made a pact to take some time to share the events of the day as soon as the kids were in bed.

Sarah shared at the dinner table how proud she was of Carson for asking his teacher if he could sit somewhere else in the classroom, so he wouldn't be tempted to talk with his friend during class.

"You must have been a little bit nervous about doing that, sweetheart," Sarah said, "but you asked for what you wanted and you took responsibility for making a change. That took courage! I loved watching you talk to her."

Carson beamed. "Yeah! Ms. Pease let me change seats. And she's going to change everyone's seats around, not just ours. So Jay won't think I didn't want to sit by him because I don't like him or something."

Emily, who had the same teacher two years ago, added, "Ms. Pease is really nice. I liked her when I had her for first grade, too."

After dinner was cleared, homework had been checked, and the kids were in bed, Lucas and Sarah brought their glasses of wine into the den and settled next to each other on the sofa. Lucas said, "Well, I saw Ted again late today. It was nice timing, too, because I had a couple of small triumphs at work today and I was able to thank him for his help. He seemed pleased to see it was having an impact. And then Ted told me some great new stuff about how to make shifts happen." Lucas filled in a few details about his day at work, and Sarah smiled broadly.

"Wow, big day! You and Carson both went for it. Would you mind going over what Ted showed you today?"

"Sure. I was afraid you wouldn't ask." Lucas grinned. He drew the diagram showing the choice point at the intersection of the DDT and TED* roles.

Sarah said, "Hmm. This diagram forms an asterisk, just like the asterisk that appears after TED*. I wonder if that means anything."

"I hadn't thought about that," said Lucas. He slid his arm around Sarah's shoulder, and she leaned her head against him and sighed.

"You know," she said, "this Ted guy is like a sage in the body of a custodian. I'm so glad the two of you struck up a conversation that night. I mean, what if you hadn't? We would've missed out on learning all this. I can already see a difference when you get home at the end of the day— you seem calmer. When the kids were sharing tonight, I could tell you were really listening. I think they may have noticed a difference, too."

"Thanks, honey," Lucas responded. "I do feel different. And it's great you're interested in trying this stuff out with me. Thanks for that." He smiled, then added, "Of course, I do still feel victimized by my job occasionally. Hopefully that'll change in time."

"I'm sure it will," Sarah said, attempting to stifle a yawn. "Before we turn in, I just want to say how grateful I am that we've agreed to raise Emily and Carson as Creators. I've been thinking about it all day, from when we talked with Carson at breakfast up until I watched him walk right up and talk to his teacher at school this afternoon. It's exciting to take what we're learning from your talks with Ted, and really apply it to our parenting."

"I think we took a great baby step in that direction this morning," said Lucas.

A Daily Practice

When Lucas checked his voicemail the next morning, he had a new message from Kasey: "Hi, Lucas. Nice to hear from you, and it's great to hear your excitement, too. If it works with your schedule, how about meeting up at my office toward the end of the day, either today or tomorrow, so we can visit a while? Just shoot me an email and let me know which day you'll drop by. I'm looking forward to it." Lucas knew Sarah would be taking the kids clothes shopping today and it would be a pizza night. He sat down and emailed Kasey suggesting four o'clock for their get-together. Within seconds, Kasey shot back a cheery "See you then!"

It was a team huddle day, and soon Lucas's four analysts gathered around his cubicle for a check-in on various projects. Lucas shared with them the outcome of yesterday's meeting with his boss and peers. Everyone in the group liked the idea of a consistent format for the analysis reports they were writing, and Lucas assured them he would ask for their input as the plan developed.

The day was remarkably drama-free. Lucas started to schedule the first meeting of the volunteers who would develop the new standard report template. To begin getting input on what the commercial banking group needed from Lucas's team's regular reports, Lucas met with one of the group's senior managers.

Later that afternoon, Lucas arrived at Kasey's office. The door was open, and he stuck his head in. "Is this still a good time for a chat?" he said.

"You bet," said Kasey. "Come on in. Just give me a minute to finish up this email."

Lucas looked around the office. He noticed a large whiteboard mounted above a small round table with four chairs. On one side of the whiteboard were drawings of the two FISBEs—the Problem/Victim Orientation and the Outcome/Creator Orientation—and below them, the DDT and TED* triangles. A line was drawn separating the diagrams from the rest of the whiteboard, and next to it, the words *DO NOT ERASE.*

Kasey sent her email and swiveled around to see Lucas looking at the whiteboard. She smiled. "Recognize those, do you? I've had them up there for a long time now. I must refer to those diagrams ten times a week, in one meeting or another. And I like having them in sight when I'm on a conference call or having a tough conversation on the phone. It helps me keep perspective."

Lucas smiled. "That's a great idea. I think I'll draw a smaller version and tack it on the wall at my desk."

Kasey stood up. "Why don't we sit down and talk a while, Lucas," she said, motioning to one of the chairs at the round table.

He'd spotted a picture of Kasey's teenage kids and her husband on her credenza. They stood in a happy swimsuited bunch, arm in arm on a beach with a bright sky and ocean waves in the background. Lucas pointed. "That picture of your family reminds me of meeting you all at the neighborhood picnic last summer."

They stood looking at the photo a minute. Kasey said, "I love that picture."

She continued. "It's been a couple of years since I started to have those life-changing talks with Ted, when he was the custodian on my floor. What Ted taught me has made a huge difference in my leadership and management style, but it's also made a real difference at home.

"The teenage years can be especially challenging," she said. "I wish I could say it's all been sweetness and light—it hasn't—but being parents and trying to co-create together and see our kids as Creators really has its rewards and breakthroughs. We try to coach instead of rush in and rescue. And we try to be Challengers when it's called for, although our kids sometimes react to that as if we were being Persecutors.

"Anyway," said Kasey, turning toward Lucas, "my life is very different because of Ted."

Lucas nodded. "Sarah and I have been talking about the

idea of parenting in that way, with empowerment instead of drama. She thinks Ted is a sage disguised as a custodian!"

Kasey smiled broadly. "I'll tell you a secret. I think of Ted as a caretaker of souls. I actually looked up the word *custodian* once—it means a person responsible to look after something. Another word for custodian is *guardian*."

Lucas let the word soak in. He certainly felt Ted was on his side. Lately it felt as if Ted was looking out for his whole family.

"Amen to that," was all Lucas could think to say. He reached for a chair and sat down, Kasey sitting across from him.

After a pause, Kasey said, "So, neighbor, what's the latest you've learned from our sage custodian?" They both laughed.

Lucas reached for his journal and opened it to the notes he'd jotted down the night before. "Last night Ted was talking about how to make the shift from the DDT roles to the TED* roles—from drama to empowerment." He laughed a little. "I feel like such a beginner telling you this. You seem to have it so together." He waved at the diagrams on Kasey's office whiteboard. "You must practice being a Creator, Challenger, and Coach—operating from a Creator Orientation—all the time."

Kasey laughed out loud. "I wish I could say that was true, Lucas! But you're right that I'm always, or at least usually, trying to practice the mindset and roles. And *practicing* really is the operative word here. Practice, not perfection. I'm convinced that, as human beings, we will always go reactive at times and find ourselves enmeshed in the DDT. But we can make it our daily practice to stay focused on outcomes and to show up in our relationships as Creators, Challengers, and Coaches as much as we possibly can.

"In fact," Kasey continued, "when I first started talking with Ted, I didn't initially identify with the Victim role. I thought others around me were acting like Victims, but not me. I was in the executive leadership development program, after all, and thought I was doing well—until I had that experience with the new-employee orientation project.

"Remember when I told you about the feedback I received on the Leadership Circle Profile? After we received that feedback, they did this great thing: they paired us up with a learning buddy—someone also going through the program. Over several months and more than a few conversations with Darryl, my learning buddy, I shared what I'd learned from Ted and we really became Coaches and Challengers for each other."

"Kind of like you're doing for me?" Lucas asked.

"Sort of. It was more intense, though, because we held each other accountable and didn't hesitate to challenge each other, as long as we were doing so from a learning intent.

"And one day we had one of those conversations. Frankly, it was back when I was reporting to the boss you have now, and I was whining about something or other. I made a comment about how I hoped he would be transferred or that someone would intervene or that he would get the kind of feedback that would make him see his impact on other people." Kasey grimaced.

"Darryl let me vent for a while," she said. "He just listened. Then he said to me, 'Sounds like you're looking for a Rescuer.' It was a profound Challenger observation. But he wasn't judging me, he was just making that observation. And I admitted it: I probably was looking for a Rescuer. Then he asked me a question that really shifted something for me."

"What did he ask you?" asked Lucas.

"He followed up that Challenger statement with a great Coach question," said Kasey. "He said, 'If you're looking outside yourself for someone or something to show up as a Rescuer, what role does that leave you in?' I was stunned."

"Let me guess," Lucas interjected. "Victim?"

"That's right. I was smack-dab in the Victim role," said Kasey. "Busted!" She laughed.

"It was so clear. I could no longer deny that I, a successful team manager, enrolled in the executive leadership development program, sometimes reacted to things as a Victim. And it was in that conversation with my learning partner that I really started practicing the TED* perspectives, intentionally making shifts happen in the way that I lead, manage, and collaborate with other people."

"What happened when you started shifting?" said Lucas. He opened to a fresh page in his journal and readied his pen.

Shifting From Victim to Creator

"Once I acknowledged that even *I* could be in Victim mode," Kasey said, "it was a matter of noticing all the times that I was subtly, and even at times explicitly, looking around for a Rescuer.

"I started to notice that whenever I experienced problems, and fell into reacting to them, my go-to strategy was often to draw others—whether direct reports, my manager, or others—into the problem. I would fool myself that I was addressing the problem by adding more people—and more drama—to the situation. I began to see that I was feeling victimized by the mess of the moment, and that I was adding to the drama rather than taking action to resolve the issue.

"So, that's when I put the drawings up." Kasey motioned to her whiteboard. "When a problem or issue arose, I would look up at that Creator FISBE and ask myself, 'What is the outcome I want, and how do I choose to respond?' I found that checking in on my inner state was also useful. I would reflect on why I cared about the challenge I was facing."

Lucas added, "Kind of like finding the commitment behind the complaint?"

"Exactly. Ted's taught you well," said Kasey. "Sometimes looking at my inner state helped me clarify what I wanted. Once I had that clarity, I could make a better choice about how to respond to the issue.

"Other times, I realized that I really didn't care about the issue. Usually that was when someone came to me with a problem that was causing *them* to feel anxiety and to react. In those cases, I could either move into the Coach role and help the other person clarify the outcome or choice *they* wanted to make. Or I might move into being a Challenger—by challenging their assumption that the issue needed an immediate response.

"If they determined it was really important to them, and that a response was urgently needed, I would stay in the TED* roles and support them to co-create *their* response. And that allowed me to stay in a Coach or a Challenger role much more of the time."

Lucas had been quickly jotting notes as Kasey shared her experience. "This is *so* helpful, Kasey! It sounds like you would support the other person in how they reacted to the problem."

Reframing Problems to Outcomes

"Not exactly, Lucas," Kasey said. "I wouldn't join them in reacting." She shifted in her chair. "To do that would keep us both stuck in the Victim Orientation. Instead I want to help people move away from focusing on what they don't want, from those desperate attempts to make the problem go away. I really want to support them in shifting to focus on an outcome they care about—one they can move toward."

As he listened, Lucas had been thinking of the many times he'd made a problem worse by focusing solely on trying to solve it. He tried to imagine what it would look like, and what it might feel like, to move toward the outcome instead. "How would you do that?" Lucas asked.

"I used a powerful technique I picked up from my learning buddy—something he in turn picked up from a professional coach he once worked with. It's called 'problem reframing.' You do this mostly from the role of Coach. You begin by asking the person what it is about the problem that they care about.

"Let's take an example. One of the departments that reports to me is Collections—the folks who have to contact customers who are behind in their payments on loans or credit cards. One day the supervisor of the Collections group came to me after receiving an email from our director. The email had pointed out the poor percentage of collections her team was getting and demanded to know how they were going to solve that problem.

"You see, another aspect of that particular problem is that, when Collections can't get a customer to pay, the account ends up being turned over to a collection agency. That, in turn, costs the bank money and also probably results in losing a customer. So there's loss involved all around."

Lucas said, "One of my team members provides the data analysis that probably led to that email from your Collections director."

"Is that right? We're all connected here, aren't we?" Kasey smiled.

Then she continued, "Well, this supervisor was quite distraught and feared she might lose her job. I wanted to help her reframe that problem she was feeling reactive about, into some kind of an outcome she cared about creating.

"I asked her a few coaching questions about what the ideal outcome of a debt collection process would be—for her, for her team, for the bank, *and* for the customer. After some discussion, she realized the ideal outcome would be a customer feeling respected and agreeing to a plan to pay off the debt. She wanted the customer to have an interaction with us that would encourage them to keep their account in good standing over time.

"So, Lucas, do you see how she shifted from focusing on what she didn't want, in reaction to the problem, and how together we reframed her challenge into an outcome she felt good about?" Kasey asked.

"Yes, I do. You must have felt good about the way you handled the situation with her. I can only hope to do that myself someday," said Lucas.

"Just keep practicing!" Kasey said cheerfully.

"Sure thing," said Lucas. "How did it turn out, if I can ask?"

"Let me tell you about the rest of my conversation with the supervisor, and then I'll fill you in on the end of the story," said Kasey.

"I showed her the Dreaded Drama Triangle on this whiteboard and asked her which roles she was playing. She was able to see how both the bank and the customer felt like Victims and saw each other as Persecutors. Customers felt the bank was persecuting them by sending letters and calling them with escalating demands for repayment. And the bank perceived the customers as Persecutors for not paying their bills."

"Then who was the Rescuer?" Lucas asked.

"Great question. That's where the real shift happened in the conversation. What we realized was that the collection agency—the one we would end up turning overdue accounts over to—was *our* Rescuer. The agency would then become the new Persecutor to the customer, especially because collection agencies are usually even more demanding than our folks."

"It's no wonder people wouldn't want to be our customers after that," Lucas agreed.

"Exactly," said Kasey. "So next, the supervisor and I explored together how we might shift the dynamic into the TED* roles. We began by seeing the customer as neither Victim nor Persecutor, but instead seeing and treating them as a Creator—someone who would welcome support in making good on their debts and avoiding a downgraded credit rating." Kasey pointed to the roles on the board as she spoke.

"After we reached that realization," Kasey continued, "I challenged her to come up with a new plan based on the Outcome Orientation and the TED* roles. She came back a couple of weeks later with an awesome approach! Through letters and calls, Collections would respectfully approach the customers and offer to help them work out a mutually agreeable plan to help them protect their credit rating. She then trained her people to really act as Coaches to our customers. As they started to treat the customers as Creators, they found that sometimes the customers actually hadn't fully understood the collection process or the consequences of defaulting on their loan or credit card. Of course, there were times one of our collectors would have to be a Challenger with a Creator-customer, but they did their challenging from a learning intention, not by putting the customer down.

"So to answer your earlier question, Lucas: our collection rate has more than *doubled* in the past year, and our rate of turning accounts over to the collection agency is way, way down."

"That's awesome," said Lucas. "I can see how the shift can result in a totally different outcome. Yesterday I had a little experience with making a shift from problem to outcome, too. Believe it or not, it happened with my boss in his staff meeting."

"Really?" Kasey said. "I'd love to hear about that."

Lucas then recounted his story of his boss focusing on the problems with their data analysis reports being inconsistent and sometimes incomplete, and not providing the bank's internal customers what they most needed.

"At first, I felt like a Victim, listening to him talk about every little detail in our reports that needed fixing. But then, once I realized that was his focus, I spoke up and asked a few questions to clarify what he really wanted. Then I volunteered to organize a small group to recommend a consistent report template that would meet most of our users' needs as he'd described them."

"Good work, Lucas!" Kasey smiled and gave him a thumbs-up. "Did he go for it?"

"He sure did," said Lucas. "I've already started talking to some department heads about their needs and have called the first meeting of the volunteer group for next week."

"That's great," said Kasey, adding, "Hey, I'd be happy to offer input on that project at some point, if you'd like. Not right now, though. I'm enjoying our conversation too much."

Kasey looked at her watch—it was five fifteen, Lucas saw. Leaving now would land them in the heart of rush-hour traffic.

"I don't know what your time is like right now, Lucas, but if you're up for it, we could head down to the lobby and over to that pub next door," Kasey said. "Would you be up for having a glass of wine or a beer and continuing our conversation? Frank is out with his buddies watching a basketball game, so my slate is clean for a little while longer. And I'm not in any hurry to jump into rush hour."

"Perfect," said Lucas. "Sarah and the kids are out shopping, and she was going to get them pizza. Let me text her what I'm up to and let her know I'll grab a bite to eat on my own."

Lucas took out his phone. Before sending the text off to his wife, he took a picture of the drawings on Kasey's whiteboard and attached it to his message.

Rescuer to Coach: Lessons Learned

The pub wasn't too noisy yet. Lucas and Kasey found a booth away from the happy hour crowd and ordered their drinks. Kasey said, "Let's talk about the Rescuer-to-Coach shift. Are you getting into that one yet?"

"Yes, that's one I've been experimenting with." Lucas took a sip of his IPA. He shared with Kasey how he had worked with the analyst on his team. Lucas admitted that in the past, he would have taken the report from the analyst, edited it himself, and added his own recommendations. Yesterday, he had shifted into more of a Challenger role by having his teammate take the initiative to revise the report.

"Now that I'm describing it, I guess that was actually more of a Rescuer-to-Challenger shift. But when I shared it with Ted, he made it clear that any shift from a DDT role into one of the TED* roles was fair game."

"Absolutely," said Kasey. "Any shift that takes us out of being a contributor to drama and into being a force for empowerment—that's what it's all about. Since I met Ted, probably the biggest change for me is making it a practice to 'ask first, tell second.'"

"I remember Ted referring to that as a mantra." Lucas said. "It sounded a little extreme at the time, but I'm starting to see how powerful that one practice could be."

"It *is* a mantra," Kasey said, "in that I need to repeat it to myself a lot!" She laughed. "When I reflect on how I used to support my direct reports, I've been amazed to see how many times I would default to being a Rescuer in various ways. Sometimes I'd intervene when they hadn't even asked me to, offering my advice or telling them I'd take care of something for them.

"Most of the time I'd do it out of enthusiasm and wanting to help. Someone would come into my office with a problem or an issue and ask what I thought they should do. My natural response would be to say, 'If I were you . . . ,' and then list three or four ideas of what I would do before asking what *they* thought their options were. That's a 'tell first, ask second' approach.

"Once I flipped that around and asked for their thoughts first, I found they often had many of the same ideas I had. And sometimes they had other ideas that were way more innovative! Once they shared their thoughts, if I had anything to add, I would share that with them. The change was incredible.

"My direct reports left my office with a spring in their step and a new sense of motivation because they were on their way to implementing their own solutions. And I was happy to have the chance to complement, reinforce, and, sometimes, add to those solutions to make them a little more effective. I wonder how many times, during the days when I defaulted to sharing my ideas first, people just never mentioned their creative inspirations and instead just did what I told them to do."

"Yeah. Makes you think, doesn't it? That's really helpful, Kasey," said Lucas. "You know, when I challenged my guy to add his own ideas to his report, he actually thanked me! I can see what you mean about motivation."

Kasey nodded and took a sip of her wine. "And one

other thing. I got a good look at the shadow side of being a Rescuer."

"What do you mean?" asked Lucas.

"I'm sure there were times when I intervened or took something over for someone—especially if they hadn't asked me to—that, even though I was trying to be helpful, the other person actually saw me as controlling, more like a Persecutor."

"I don't quite understand," said Lucas. "How could you land in the role of Persecutor if you were sincerely trying to help them?"

"One of the written comments I got in my Leadership Circle feedback was that sometimes people felt put down when I took over a problem from them. In a sense, they felt I was implying they weren't capable, or that I knew better. It was a little embarrassing to uncover that shadow side, seeing that my 'help' wasn't always helpful."

Lucas looked at his glass of beer. He wondered what blind spots his own experiments with the TED* roles might reveal. "I really appreciate you being so candid, Kasey, and sharing all of this with me. It gives me a lot to think about with my team. I think it's going to be especially useful once I'm in a more official leadership position. This is one time when your help has definitely been helpful!"

"Thanks, Lucas. And you're welcome," Kasey said. "Also, I want to remind you that actually, you already *are* in a leadership position. I think there's an important difference between management . . . and leadership.

"Management is a role, a formal position you can point

to on an organization chart that shows who reports to whom. Leadership, on the other hand, is something that everyone is capable of. It doesn't need to be official. You lead your team of analysts. Each of those analysts leads in the way they interact with their internal clients and with one another. And if you want to know the truth, I think Ted's 3 Vital Questions have a lot more to do with leadership than they have to do with management."

"Hmm," said Lucas. "So you're both a leader and a manager in your position."

"Well, I like to think so, anyway!" Kasey smiled. "But I'll be practicing that leadership and those 3 Vital Questions for the rest of my career—the rest of my life, for that matter.

"Oh, and one last thing about the shift from Rescuer to Coach, while we're on the subject," Kasey added. "Did Ted mention to you what he calls the *internal shift*?"

"He sure did," Lucas chimed in, glad to be asked. "Let me see if I got what Ted told me about that kind of shift. That's about shifting the way I look at my experience, right?"

"Right on—and it's a tricky one for us recovering Rescuers." Kasey chuckled. "Very often a Rescuer is so focused on taking care of others that they either don't take care of themselves or they don't ask for support when they need it. Self-care doesn't always come easy.

"I remember this one time, I decided I would pamper myself by getting a massage at the gym. The irony was that the whole time I was lying on that table, I couldn't stop thinking about other people and all the things I needed to do for them! I've really had to work on taking time for myself, to recharge."

"What have you done?" asked Lucas.

"For one thing, I've scheduled massages every other Saturday morning. And during the massage, I try not to think about anything at all," said Kasey. "I also started a daily practice doing a little bit of meditation and taking some quiet time every morning. Of course, it helps that I have teenagers who can fend for themselves and get ready for school on their own.

"The other thing I've learned—and this is a hard one," said Kasey, "is to ask for help or support when I need it. Habitual Rescuers like ourselves tend to see asking for help as a sign of weakness, or as though somehow by asking for support they're becoming a Victim. Now, I'm not talking about asking someone to rescue me. But let's say I need help on a project. Asking someone who has the expertise I need isn't weakness, it's wisdom. Pulling in the right person to make the project the best it can be—that's an act of leadership I can feel good about. And I'm grateful to have my learning buddy, Darryl, to bounce ideas off of. I can always ask him to serve as a Coach when I'm uncertain or struggling. Sometimes I'll go to a direct report or to my boss to help me think through something, or ask for their perspective, knowing that the final choice about what I'll do is still mine to make."

Persecutor to Challenger: Lessons Learned

Kasey finished her last sip of wine and looked at her watch. "This has been so great, Lucas. I probably should get going in a few minutes. Before I do, are you interested in talking a little about the Persecutor-to-Challenger shift?"

"Absolutely! I'm all ears," said Lucas.

"I've learned to pause before I step into the Challenger role and ask myself, 'What is my intention behind this challenge?'" said Kasey. "I ask myself, 'Am I coming from a learning intention or a "looking good" intention?' To be a conscious and constructive Challenger, I have to come from an intention to learn.

"Any time my intention is merely to look good, it's almost certain my words or actions will be perceived and reacted to as those of a Persecutor. Some of the ways I attempt to look good are when I assertively try to show I'm right and the other person is wrong—they usually see that as me being critical. It was a blow to my ego to realize, when I got my Leadership Circle feedback, that there were times this was true. Sometimes when I jumped into a situation as a Rescuer—trying to be the hero and save the day—it was also a way of making myself look good and one-upping those around me. Looking good based on a judgment that 'I know best' and that, therefore, I have a right to control things. It was pretty embarrassing to see that about myself."

"Well, thanks for being so honest," said Lucas. "It's brave of you, and I appreciate it. Do you mind me asking how you can tell when you're coming from a learning intent, though?"

Kasey said, "It starts with pausing and being certain that the focus is on learning, whether for an individual or a team. The intention needs to be to foster learning and growth and to increase the capabilities, competencies, and capacities of others. And it's done with respect and care, and even compassion, at times, especially when the learning isn't easy or is even painful in some way. If I see that I'm not coming from that place, I try to adjust."

"I remember Ted saying something about compassion being important as a Challenger," Lucas added.

"Yes, and he probably emphasized that a Challenger is a truth teller," said Kasey. "I've learned to share with people what I'm noticing or feeling in a situation, but doing it without attaching any blame or judgment. In fact, speaking my truth this way can open the door for others to share their own perceptions, observations, and feelings. And when they do, I try to stay open and listen for possibilities in what they say. I try to stay open to being influenced or changing my opinion as a result. It does take practice.

"Another thing that has spurred my growth as a Challenger is to bring assumptions to the surface and challenge them. It's amazing how often we'll make a decision to go down a certain path without looking at the assumptions that led up to it.

"I told you about the situation with the Collections supervisor and how she turned the situation around with such great results. Part of what unlocked her new approach was that we really looked together at our assumption that the customers who were involved in the collections process were somehow Victims or else deserved to be there. We challenged that assumption when we started treating them as Creators we could work with—people who would naturally want to clear up their situation with the bank."

Lucas added, "I'll bet those customers would say the Collections folks were being Challengers, not Persecutors, if they knew those terms."

"I'd like to think so." Kasey smiled. "And I think the results of our new, more respectful approach reflect that we're on the right track. Getting clear about our assumptions is powerful, and can often lead to those kinds of breakthroughs. Every time we can identify an assumption, we've given ourselves the choice to either reaffirm that assumption as valid, or to reframe it or revise it. And sometimes we decide to retire it . . . because it's no longer an assumption that serves the situation."

Kasey glanced at her watch again. "Oops, now I really do need to go. You're learning a lot from Ted, Lucas. I've been impressed with your grasp of everything we've been talking about."

Lucas sat back in his seat. "Thanks, Kasey. The past few days have shown me what a big impact this stuff can have on, well, really any situation that comes along. And your sharing with me how you apply what you've learned from Ted is definitely reinforcing that reality! So again, thanks—and the drinks are on me."

"Thanks!" said Kasey, standing up and grabbing her briefcase. "You ready to go?"

"No," said Lucas. "I told Sarah I'd grab a bite to eat, so I'm going to order a sandwich and do some journaling. You've given me a lot to think about."

"I look forward to more of these conversations, Lucas. See you." Kasey said, and she headed for the door.

VITAL 3 QUESTION

What actions are you taking?

CHAPTER TEN

What Actions Are You Taking?

I t had been nearly a month since Lucas had seen Ted. In that time, he'd found the new ways of thinking and relating he had learned were not only more satisfying, but made him surprisingly efficient at work. He now was able to go home on schedule most evenings. And Sarah and the kids were happy about that, too.

However, as Kasey had warned, all was not "sweetness and light."

For instance, Thursday morning, Lucas received an email from a senior manager in the Mortgage Lending Department about a data analysis report that hadn't arrived.

Breakdowns

When Lucas followed up with the analyst responsible for the missing report, his teammate said that sending the report had "slipped my mind."

Lucas had gone reactive. He called the analyst irresponsible and careless and said he couldn't tolerate such sloppy work. He ordered his team member to email the manager immediately and set up a time to talk in person, to apologize and expedite the client's request. Lucas had also told the analyst to copy him and his boss on the email. The last thing Lucas wanted was for his boss to find out about the slipup indirectly.

That night, Lucas arrived home in a sour mood.

As dinner baked in the oven and the kids played in the backyard, he and Sarah sat down to watch the evening news together. A news story came on about Lucas's least favorite politician, and Lucas made a sarcastic statement about all the damage he felt the guy was doing.

Sarah said simply, "Pass." That was a surprise!

Lucas looked at her, stunned. "What do you mean, 'pass'?"

"Well, I agree with you," Sarah said. "And in the past, I'd typically say something that would reinforce how we both see him as a Persecutor. But that would place us both in the DDT, so this time I decided to pass instead of going there." She smiled.

Lucas muted the TV and turned to Sarah. "Wow. Good move, sweetie! I guess there are times when just not getting pulled into a drama is an empowered move in and of itself. I've been really focusing on the shift between the FISBEs and the DDT and TED* roles, but I've been missing the option to just 'pass' on the drama."

Lucas went on to tell Sarah about his encounter with the analyst on his team. "I was kicking myself all the way home about how I should have been more of a Challenger instead of being such a Persecutor. I was really triggered, and I reacted because of my concern about looking good. I was thinking it was a step backward, after all the work I've been doing to create a better relationship with my boss. I knew I would have to make him aware of the situation, and I really dreaded him seeing the mistake."

Sarah took his hand and said, "At least you didn't react by taking over as a Rescuer. Then you would have stayed late at the office, like you have so many times in the past. I know there'll be other times when you have to work late, but I've really liked having you home before dinner, like you were tonight."

In the kitchen, the oven timer went off: *beep-beep-beep.* Dinner was about ready. As Sarah got up, Lucas turned off the TV. He remembered a phrase from the game show *Family Feud* in which contestants were asked to "pass or play." That Sarah. He chuckled. She had chosen to pass instead of playing into the DDT. One less drama!

Lucas joined Sarah in the kitchen, making a mental note to connect soon with his team member on a more positive note. The mood was light as he and Sarah set the table and set out the meal. Lucas called for the kids come in and wash up before they all sat down. It was good to be home.

Breakthroughs

While Lucas's new way of approaching situations had led to a few setbacks, there had also been times when he felt encouraged, when he reaped the benefits of applying what he'd been learning from Ted and Kasey. Among a few triumphant moments, one episode in particular stood out.

Several weeks ago, to support his choice to create a better working relationship with his boss, Lucas had asked if the two of them could meet one-on-one for thirty minutes every two weeks.

"Why would you want to do that?" his boss asked. "I think we should meet when an issue arises, or I need to delegate something. You know, meet when we really need to." The look on his face was far from encouraging.

Lucas had anticipated the reply, given how problem-focused his boss seemed to be. He only called meetings when there was a problem to react to. Lucas's intent was to bring a more outcome-oriented focus to their work relationship, and he was prepared to be a stealth Challenger to his boss.

"Certainly, there are times when something unforeseen comes up that we need to talk about," Lucas said. "That said, I would like us to meet regularly so I can keep you up to date on projects and client requests, or ask for your input. My hope is that this might reduce the number of unanticipated issues we both have to react to. I want to be more proactive in my role as team lead."

Lucas's boss leaned back in his chair and looked up as he pondered the request. "I see your point, Lucas. Let's give it a shot."

"Great! How about I take responsibility for bringing the agenda items for our meetings? Of course, if there are things you want to talk about that aren't on my list, we would make time for those, too."

"I like that even better," his boss said, standing to indicate that this meeting was ending. "Let's consider this our first such meeting. Send me a request for another one a couple of weeks out, and we'll get thirty minutes on the calendar."

They had an agreement. And Lucas had taken the first step to make it happen. It felt like a breakthrough.

Last week, Lucas and his boss had logged their first official meeting. During the half-hour, Lucas reported that the work developing the consistent report template was progressing well, but that the team needed more time to gather additional input from clients as well as from some of the analysts who would be writing the reports.

"I gave you all a whole month to do this project," his boss reacted, his face reddening. "That should have been plenty of time! I told my boss I would have the new template ready for her review in thirty days, and she's expecting to see it by Wednesday."

Lucas felt a bit flustered, but he was determined. Instead of reacting to his boss's reaction by defending himself, he paused. He quietly took a deep breath, grounded himself, and mentally "went up to the balcony" to get perspective on what was going on. He quickly realized that his boss most likely feared looking bad to *his* boss if he had to go to her with the news that the report wasn't ready on time. He was feeling like a Victim.

Lucas then offered, "Would it help if I shot you an email with an update of what we've gathered so far, and what the group is thinking? I would also include reasons why we need another week or so to deliver a more complete report and recommendations."

His boss took a deep breath and let out a big sigh. "Okay, Lucas. That would be helpful," he said, visibly relaxing a bit. "Then I can forward her the email with my comments."

Lucas left the meeting pondering that exchange. He asked himself, "Was I being a Rescuer just then?" But he realized that, no, he had offered the suggestion not as a Rescuer, but as a Co-Creator of the positive outcome he and his boss both wanted—a new, consistent reporting template. "Score one for The Empowerment Dynamic!" he said to himself as he headed back to his cubicle.

"Pass or Play"

By the time Lucas got back to his office, it was the end of the normal workday. He decided to text Sarah that he needed to stay late to write an email to his boss, that he should be home by dinnertime, and to call if she needed anything. He added a smile-and-kiss emoji before sending it.

Just as Lucas was finishing the email to his boss, the door opened at the end of the corridor. He heard Ted's cleaning cart squeaking through the maze of cubicles, accompanied by the custodian's gentle humming. Several minutes later, Ted had made his way to Lucas's workspace.

"Why, hello, young man!" Ted said when he spied Lucas at his desk. "I've wondered where you've been. Thought maybe you had been promoted or took a new job, but I knew you were still around because all your pictures and things were still here. How've you been?" Ted parked his cart alongside the partition.

"Overall, things have been going really well," said Lucas. "Not perfect, but pretty well."

"Progress, not perfection, is the way forward, my friend!" said Ted. "This way of thinking, relating, and taking action is a lifelong journey. I can attest to that in my own life.

"So, tell me what's been going on. That is, if you have the time."

Lucas poured out how he had been experimenting with staying in the outcome-focused Creator Orientation as much as possible, and relating from the TED* roles. He admitted that he still found himself getting triggered and going reactive at times. He told Ted about his meeting with his teammate the day before, when he had reacted from the DDT as a Persecutor.

"Ah, a backward baby step." Ted nodded. "That happens."

"What do you mean, a 'backward baby step'?" said Lucas.

"I'll say more about that, maybe a little later. First I'd love to hear about any successes you've had in your experiments with the first two vital questions."

"Sure." Lucas recounted his conversation with Sarah and her "pass" response.

Ted was impressed that Sarah, too, was applying the TED* ways of thinking and relating. "She's a wise woman, Lucas! You're lucky to be with her," he said.

Lucas smiled and nodded. "I clearly married up," he said.

Ted continued, "Sarah's idea—that you can 'pass or play'—is right on the money! When faced with a drama situation—especially with another person or in a group—a Creator can always choose whether to let the drama pass them by or play into the DDT.

"Of course, there's a constructive way you could choose to play," said Ted. "You could step into a TED* role—as a Creator, Challenger, or Coach—and play with the impact, see whether this transforms the drama into a more productive interaction.

"When you and Sarah were watching that politician on TV, she avoided a common pitfall by 'passing.' She managed not to enter into what I call the 'kinship of victimhood.'"

"What's that?" asked Lucas.

"Well, I see and hear it all too frequently," said Ted. "It's when people reinforce each other in the Victim perspective. As a custodian, I overhear a lot of conversations, whether I mean to or not. And I can't tell you how many times I hear employees talking about how awful things are, as though they're trying to one-up each other in their sense of victimization. One person starts with some kind of lament, and then the other follows up with something like, 'You think that's bad. Let me tell you what happened to me that was even worse.' And it continues like that, each keeping the other going around and around in the DDT."

Lucas nodded. "Yes. I see that happening all the time around here. Since I started observing my interactions while keeping the TED* awareness, it's so obvious what a waste of time and energy it is."

"Sounds like you've been going to the balcony." Ted chimed in.

"Exactly!" said Lucas. "Kasey told me you shared that metaphor with her, and it's been really helpful to me, too. And that reminds me—I had an interesting meeting with my boss this afternoon . . ."

Lucas told Ted about pitching the idea of regular proactive meetings with his boss, and how going to the balcony had helped him avoid reacting to his boss's reaction.

"Even better," Lucas went on, "it actually made it possible for me to feel a little compassion for my boss's fear of not looking good to *his* boss. And it led to a co-creative suggestion!"

Harnessing Dynamic Tension

"Two things strike me about your story, Lucas," said Ted. "The first is how you went to the balcony and saw the fear behind your boss's reaction. That takes insight. Remember: all three roles in the DDT are fear-based. Persecutors fear their own victimization, as you saw. A Rescuer has a different fear—not being needed. And a Victim fears they can't have something they want or need.

"This brings us to the third vital question, if you're ready for it."

"You bet I am!" said Lucas, grabbing his backpack and fishing out his journal.

"The third vital question is, *What actions are you taking?*" said Ted. "If you're operating from the problem-focused

Victim Orientation and relating to others—and to your experience in general—from the DDT, the actions you take are destined to be *re*actions. That is, your actions react to the anxiety and fear you feel. You saw that happening with your boss.

"On the other hand, if you've adopted a Creator Orientation and are focused on outcomes—if you're relating to others and to your experience through the TED* roles—then the actions you take are going to be creative and generative. As you engage in creating outcomes, you also solve problems. That's what you were doing when you suggested regular, proactive meetings with your boss."

"Hmm." Lucas pondered, adding, "I guess I was offering a solution to what he saw as a problem—my asking for more time to draft the report template."

"You got it! The second thing your story shows is how we take baby steps. That suggestion you made was a baby step in the process of creating an outcome. The idea of baby steps is central to the third vital question." Ted paused and asked, "Mind if I use the whiteboard again?"

"Not at all," said Lucas. He pulled open his desk drawer and handed Ted a couple of whiteboard markers.

"The third vital question is all about harnessing the power of what's called *dynamic tension*. Dynamic tension is a universal tool for creating . . . well, *anything*, frankly, and it has three main parts."

Ted wrote the words *Outcome* near the top of the whiteboard.

"Dynamic tension always starts with a focus on the outcome you want to create," Ted explained. "You might say the outcome is your intention. Sometimes that outcome is clear and concrete, and other times it may be more vague. But you know the direction you want to be moving. As you define your outcome, here's a powerful question to ask: If your outcome were fully complete, how would you know? Another way to put it: What is your criteria for success?"

Ted paused. "What's your desired outcome for that project you're working on with your team—the one that's a little late?"

Lucas thought for a moment. "We said the outcome we want is to create a consistent template for data analysis reports—one that not only meets our clients' existing needs, but also offers them recommendations based on the data in the report."

"And if you had that project successfully completed, how would you know it? What would people be saying? What would be your evidence that the template is working the way you described?" Ted asked.

"Well," Lucas paused, then thought out loud. "First, the clients we serve would be saying that they find the reports a big help in their decision-making and that they appreciate knowing how to read the report because of the consistent format. Another thing would be that the data analysts writing the report would like it and feel empowered because we're asking them to include their recommendations—really use their data-backed knowledge. And I guess another would be that clients would actually be using the recommendations from the reports we send them."

"Nice!" said Ted. Then he turned and wrote *Current Reality* toward the bottom of the whiteboard, below *Outcome*.

"Now then," said Ted, "The second part of this three-part process of creating is to figure out what your current reality is—in relation to the outcome you're trying to create."

Ted drew a vertical line connecting *Current Reality* and *Outcome*. Turning to face Lucas, he asked, "Do you have a couple of rubber bands in that desk of yours? I could use them to illustrate something here."

"I'm sure I do . . ." said Lucas, pulling open his desk drawer. He found a fairly big blue rubber band that had come with a bundle of mail, and a smaller straw-colored one that had come with his office supplies. He handed the big one to Ted.

"There is a little more to say about this notion of current reality, and I'll come back to it in a minute," said Ted. "But first I want to show you why this"—he indicated the line he'd just drawn—"is referred to as dynamic tension. I will demonstrate by using this rubber band." He smiled broadly.

Ted turned back to the board and stretched the rubber band between the word *Outcome* and the phrase *Current Reality*.

Ted continued, "There is a tension—a force—that gets engaged between what you want, the outcome, and what you currently have, which is current reality. Use your fingers to stretch the rubber band with one end up and the other down. Do you feel the tension in the rubber band?"

"Sure!" Lucas chuckled. "Actually, I play with this rubber band a lot when I'm on a conference call, just to have something to do with my hands."

Ted nodded and smiled. "The tension you feel in that rubber band is like the creative force you harness in dynamic tension," he explained. "The principle here is that the tension between the outcome and the current reality naturally seeks to be resolved.

"But here's the kicker. When we engage this dynamic tension, we human beings often feel anxious. This anxiety comes along with the creative force of tension when we *don't know how to hold* the tension.

"So, Lucas, I want to give you a little test," said Ted with a wink. "It's related to something we talked about a little while back.

"If you feel anxiety when you're harnessing this dynamic tension—if anxiety is the inner state—which of the two FISBEs are you likely to be operating from?"

Lucas replied almost immediately, "Anxiety is the inner state of the problem-focused Victim Orientation."

"You passed! Well played, my friend," Ted said with a grin. "So, as you already know, if you have an inner state of anxiety, that's going to drive reactive behavior as you engage with the tension of creating."

"I see your point," Lucas said, frowning a little. "But why is that so important?"

"Because," Ted responded, "there are a couple of ways you might react to the anxiety you feel when you work with dynamic tension that are merely reactions to it, and these won't take you where you want to go.

"The first possible reaction: you could let go of, or compromise, your vision of the outcome. Hold your rubber band up again and engage the tension between the outcome and current reality. Now, at the top of the rubber band, where the outcome is, move your fingers down a little."

Lucas pulled the rubber band taut and moved his fingers. "Now what?" he asked.

"Notice," Ted said, "how that releases the tension but does nothing to move you toward the outcome? This reaction may cause you to let go of the outcome altogether . . . or you might settle for something less than what you really want—a compromise of sorts. And the reality is that no one wants to invest their passion in a compromise.

"The other way you could react to the anxiety you feel is to distort or misrepresent the current reality. You could minimize, deny, or explain away the anxiety—in other words, not tell the whole truth about the current situation—and, in so doing, reduce your anxiety, at least temporarily. You might say, 'It's not as bad as it seems,' or you might acknowledge only the parts of your current situation that confirm what you want to see. But that's ultimately a dangerous delusion that could lead you to miss something in the current situation that could be critically important to moving toward the outcome you want."

Lucas relaxed the rubber band. He thought of times he had wished things were different, easier—times he'd fudged his analysis or adjusted the truth to make it feel more comfortable.

"So now can you see that compromising your vision of the outcome, or not telling the truth about current reality, are really only reactions to the anxiety that comes up when you engage dynamic tension in the creating process?"

"I definitely can," said Lucas. "I can tell you, I have practice with both kinds of reactions. But how can I hold the tension and also respond to the anxiety in a constructive way?"

Ted smiled. "I'm so glad you asked that, my friend. The reality is that the process of creating is never anxiety-free. The question is, does the anxiety have you . . . or do you have the anxiety? Are you able to just feel it without having to react? That's what we have to consider.

"The key," Ted continued, "is to hold to the envisioned outcome and—very importantly—tell the whole truth to yourself and others about current reality: both what's going well and what's getting in the way or limiting your ability to bring the outcome to fruition. In other words, you want to pay attention to anything that supports your progress, as well as anything that inhibits your movement toward the outcome."

Ted wrote the words *Supports* and *Inhibits* at the bottom of the board and drew lines connecting them to *Current*

Reality. He added, "Again, whenever we're creating outcomes, it's important not to ignore the problems that exist, because solving problems is an inevitable part of the process. It's in the inhibiting aspects of current reality that we find the problems that need to be dealt with. These are the very problems you want to respond, rather than react, to. In problem solving, it's important to choose the problems that directly relate to the outcome you want to create. You want to put your time and attention on those.

"Once you've done the work of clarifying the outcome as best you can, and once you have assessed current reality in a balanced way—considering both what supports and what inhibits your progress—then you can harness the energy bound up in that dynamic tension. You do that by determining what baby steps you can take that will move you from your current reality toward the outcome."

Ted turned and drew an arrow pointing from *Current Reality* toward *Outcome.* To the right of the arrow he wrote *Baby Steps.*

"Baby steps are immediate, or at least short-term. A baby step is anything that you, or those you're working with, have the responsibility to act on. A baby step could be leveraging something that is going well and supports the outcome. Or it could mean eliminating or overcoming whatever is inhibiting your creation of the outcome. A baby step could mean scheduling a meeting or gathering information . . . or going through some kind of problem-solving process.

"And here's something else worth remembering. Every time you take a baby step, one of three things is bound to happen. One, you take the step and it results in forward progress that helps build momentum. Second, you may take a baby step that ends up being a mistake or a step back from your outcome. That's what I meant a few minutes ago, about taking a step backward. In that case, you'll want to see what that step back may tell you about how to move forward with your *next* baby step."

Ted paused, folded his arms, and leaned against the whiteboard.

Lucas had been listening intently. "I thought you said that one of three things would happen. What's the third option?"

"Third: you never know when a baby step is going to be a breakthrough or a quantum leap—something that never would have happened had you not taken that step," said Ted. "This is where synchronicity and serendipity can show up. You take action, you take your baby step, and something totally unexpected shows up to support your movement toward the outcome."

"Interesting," was all that Lucas could think to say. "I can see why you said baby steps are so integral to creating outcomes."

Ted pointed to the whiteboard. "So there you have it, the three-step process—you might say the three-step dance—of creating. First, focus on what you want—the outcome. Second, pay attention to what you have now—the current reality. And third, take the baby step. You then continue the three-step dance as you keep getting closer to, and clearer about, the outcome you're after.

Diagram 12. Dynamic Tension

"Pick up the rubber band again, Lucas," said Ted, "and stretch it between your fingers to represent the tension between your desired outcome and your current reality. Now, move your 'current reality' fingers at the bottom toward the outcome at the top. See how you're resolving the tension by taking baby steps from the current reality toward your vision, your outcome?"

"Yes, I see that," said Lucas as he played with the rubber band.

"That's how you harness dynamic tension to create outcomes and achieve results," said Ted.

Lucas finished drawing the dynamic tension diagram in his journal. "This would have been really helpful when we started working on the data analyst report template.

At the same time, we kind of followed the steps you just described."

Lucas continued, "I did share with the group the FISBE of the Outcome/Creator Orientation, and then we started by defining what we wanted to create. Although we didn't use the same language, we looked at the various ways that different groups have produced reports and picked some of the best elements from a few of them. So I guess you could say we were determining the supports in current reality."

"Sounds about right to me," said Ted.

Lucas went on, "As a group, we realized there were several assumptions we had been making about what our internal clients wanted and needed. I would call those inhibitors, since we didn't know for certain what they actually wanted.

"And since then we've taken quite a few baby steps. We've been meeting with clients to get input on what they want, and now that's pretty much completed. At the last meeting, though, we realized we hadn't asked the analysts themselves for input, which definitely could have inhibited them really taking on the final template and using it. That was a bit of a step back, given the timeline we had agreed to. That's why I asked my boss for more time. So now we've decided to run a draft of the template by some of the analysts, to get their input. We meet next week to pull together their input and finalize the template."

"Excellent example," Ted said, handing Lucas the markers. "In some ways, you automatically harness dynamic tension whenever you're creating something. However, making it a conscious process—really knowing you're doing that three-step dance—can be useful in so many situations.

"Just a couple more things to keep in mind when you use this process deliberately. First, always, always, *always* start with the outcome. What's great about your example is that you didn't assume you all knew what the outcome should be, before you had all the information you needed.

"The second thing is, when you're assessing current reality—especially if you're brainstorming with a group— always start with supports before going to inhibitors."

"Why is that?" said Lucas.

"A couple of reasons. One, you may be surprised how many things are already going well and supporting the outcome. Seeing this builds positive energy. People usually want to jump immediately into working on the problems and inhibitors. But if you start with identifying inhibitors, it can make it harder to shift over to consider the positives. Again, it's an energy thing."

Ted reached down and picked up Lucas's wastebasket. He emptied it into the large trash bag in his cart. "I think you'll find all kinds of ways to use this three-step process, Lucas," he said, smiling. "All kinds of ways."

Then he said, "Well, I've got to go and finish my rounds. I hope you can put into practice the 3 Vital Questions we've talked about. Actually, it sounds like you're well on your way, my friend. I've really enjoyed our conversations. I feel lucky to have had this chance to share what I learned from that CEO years ago. Keeps me young. It's one of the benefits of being a custodian, if you know what I mean."

"You're a custodian, all right," said Lucas as he slipped his journal back into his backpack. "Not only do you keep my work environment running well, you've kept me from feeling like a Victim in my job. I can't thank you enough, Ted."

"That's what I'm here for," Ted said as he put his hand on the cleaning cart and resumed his path down the corridor. "Keep up the good work, Lucas!" he called.

"You bet!" Lucas answered.

Lucas turned to his computer. He was about to shut it down for the night, but then paused. He wrote an email to the analyst he had come down on that morning. In it, Lucas apologized for his reaction and said he would like to meet sometime on Monday to talk about the best way to move forward.

With that, Lucas shut down his laptop and headed home full of wonder about all he had learned through the kindness of Ted.

CHAPTER ELEVEN

Applying Dynamic Tension

Saturday was one of those days Lucas loved most. The kids ran in circles on the new spring grass, barely avoiding the colorful new pink and yellow tulips and daffodils at the edge of the flower bed. Lucas and Sarah relaxed on the patio, enjoying a glass of lemonade. They'd been looking forward to this weekend, and to doing some dreaming together about a few home improvements.

As they watched the kids playing tag, Lucas and Sarah laughed out loud, joining the children's squeals of delight at their dodging and darting getaway maneuvers.

A rickety backyard fence had long enclosed the favorite play area for Emily, Carson, and their friends. Repairing or replacing it to ensure the kids' safety had to be a priority. This seemed the right time for a little casual brainstorming about what to do.

Lucas stood up suddenly, and Sarah smiled in anticipation.

"I just thought of something, honey," Lucas said. "Let me get my journal and show you the process Ted shared with me yesterday. It was the main point of the third vital question. Things were so hectic last night that I didn't want to get into sharing it with you then. But this would be a perfect time—we can use that process to talk about the fence."

Lucas returned with his journal. Sarah scooted her chair closer to his so she could see the dynamic tension diagram as Lucas did his best to summarize Ted's "three-step dance" of creating. As Sarah considered the drawings, Lucas sat back and breathed a sigh.

"So, what do you think?"

"I love it!" said Sarah. "Let's give it a go."

They started by brainstorming a vision of the outcome. Sarah suggested they take a step back from just focusing on the fence and ask themselves what the real outcome was. Together they decided it was to have a safe and kid-friendly backyard as part of their family environment.

A new fence was a key part of creating that outcome. The existing one was just too far gone. Sarah and Lucas agreed that they wanted a cedar fence, with a gate to the driveway. Also, they'd always imagined having a dog when the kids grew big enough to help with walking and cleaning up after a pet. So another criteria was that the fence be high enough that a full-grown Labrador retriever couldn't jump over it. Sarah said that in her envisioned outcome, the fence had a little lattice at the top. Lucas liked that idea, too.

The two moved on to discuss their current reality. The current fence was visibly sagging and leaning—and they saw this fact as a support, because it established the need for a new one. The kids loved playing in the yard and often invited their friends to play there, too. Lucas and Sarah liked the fact that their home had become a recreational hub for the neighborhood kids—this was something they wanted to continue to support. Another support: they had built up a good amount of savings.

As Sarah and Lucas talked about inhibitors to their new fence outcome, they got into more detail about finances. Relaxing on the porch without any documentation at hand, they weren't sure yet, but both assumed their savings wouldn't cover the full cost of a new fence. It was something they would have to look into more carefully—they didn't want to drain their savings account on this one project. And neither Sarah nor Lucas knew of any contractors in the area that built fences. Finally, timing was an issue. It was now early spring, and once the kids were out of school for the summer, there would be even more activity in their backyard. Lucas and Sarah wanted to replace the fence before then.

The two of them could feel the dynamic tension between their desired outcome and their current reality. They agreed that the supports outweighed the inhibitors, so they began talking about the baby steps they could take over the next two to three weeks. Sarah offered to ask a few neighbors who also had wood fences if they knew of contractors, and then to choose one or two of the contractors to contact for bids on the cost of replacing the fence.

After they had talked through the dynamic tension process, Sarah said, "That was fun, using Ted's process to think through this. You know, Lucas, we have been so fortunate in what you've learned from Ted through those three questions.

"I realized the other day I was asking myself, 'How am I relating?'—to the clerk at the drugstore. The things Ted's taught you have really made a difference in how I think about things, and just how I go through my day in general. It will be interesting to see what else comes out of your conversations with Ted."

"Yeah, it will," said Lucas, taking a sip of his lemonade. "No telling what other wisdom he may have to share. He's a wise soul, that's for sure."

And then it was dinnertime. They called the kids in. As Emily and Carson came into the house, a bit breathless from their game of tag with their friends, Emily said to her brother, "You were such a Victim when I tagged you last time!"

"Yeah? Well you were such a Persecutor always going after me!" Carson said in retort, and they both laughed.

Lucas and Sarah laughed, too. As the kids went to wash their hands, Lucas said softly, "I think we have a new family culture emerging here."

Sarah took his hand. "I think you're right, sweetie."

The Performance Review

On Monday morning, Lucas settled in at his desk and booted up his laptop. The first email that popped up was from Kasey:

"Hey Lucas, something's come up that I would really like to share with you. Do you have time to meet in the next day or two?"

Lucas quickly responded, "Sure, I could meet after 4:00 today or tomorrow after 2:00," and a few minutes later Kasey emailed back: "Perfect! Meet you at my office this afternoon."

Before heading out to meet with Kasey, Lucas went by the coffee shop. It had been a hectic day. As he rode the elevator up to Kasey's floor, he thought about his morning conversation with his data analyst.

Lucas felt pretty good about his apology for the way he'd reacted when he learned his teammate had dropped the ball on that internal report. Lucas mentally went over the steps he had taken: consciously shifting into the Challenger role, then focusing on how he could contribute to some kind of learning for the analyst's benefit.

He replayed the conversation in his mind. Lucas had said, "I realized on the drive home that when I came in and asked you about the missing report, I was actually more centered on myself than you. I was reacting to how my boss might see me, as the team lead, even though I wasn't entirely aware of that at the time. So I'm sorry I blew up."

After apologizing, Lucas had told his teammate, "That said, I was still surprised at how you seemed to shrug it off that the report had fallen off your radar. You're usually right on top of things, and I want our boss to see you in the best light. Is there a way we can set up some sort of system so this doesn't happen again?"

In the elevator, Lucas smiled, realizing that he had delivered a one-two punch of Challenger and Coach in support of his analyst.

Lucas arrived at Kasey's office and glanced through the open door. She was on the phone, so he waited a moment. When she caught sight of him, she waved him in and motioned for him to take a seat at the table.

When she ended her call, Kasey asked, "How's it been going, Lucas? Any more conversations with our friend Ted?"

"Yes, actually," said Lucas. "We met up a couple of nights ago. Ted shared with me the third vital question and told me about dynamic tension."

"Ah, what a great process!" said Kasey as she came around from behind her desk and took a chair at the table. "I've used it in so many ways, from project planning, to staff meetings, to performance review conversations."

Lucas perked up at Kasey's last example. He thought about mentioning the follow-up conversation he'd had that morning with his analyst. Instead he said, "Sarah and I practiced using it this weekend. We thought through how we're going to replace our backyard fence, following that three-step process. It was so helpful. We avoided getting lost in focusing only on the problem of how much it might cost."

"That's a good example," Kasey responded. "It's such a simple structure for developing a plan of action. But it really reduces the risk of merely reacting to the problem and the anxiety. Without a structure to follow, it's so easy to default to the Problem Orientation and go right into drama. When you start with the outcome, problems just naturally end up being addressed in service to the outcome. Not the other way around."

Lucas replied, "I think if Sarah and I had talked about replacing the fence before I met Ted and learned about the 3 Vital Questions, we would've ended up focusing on how much money it would take to do the project and all the reasons we couldn't afford it. Instead we decided on a couple of baby steps to gather information. And then hopefully we can take steps to solve the financial challenge once we know more."

Kasey noticed Lucas's cup of coffee. "Just a second," she said, getting up to retrieve her own late-afternoon cup from the credenza. Lucas's mind wandered back to his conversation with the data analyst.

"I wish I'd thought to use the dynamic tension framework with one of my analysts this morning," said Lucas. "His performance has been less than expected—he totally lost a request from one of the senior managers in Mortgage last week, but he didn't seem too concerned about it. You mentioned using the dynamic tension structure in your performance review conversations. I'm curious how you apply it in that kind of situation, if you don't mind sharing."

"Oh, sure, happy to share," Kasey said. "Actually, the kind of conversation I was referring to wasn't the formal performance review. It's how I handle a conversation in the interim when someone isn't meeting expectations."

"That's perfect for me," Lucas interjected, "As a team lead, I don't conduct formal performance appraisals, I only provide input to my boss for him to use. But of course I still need to talk with people about how they're doing."

"Right. Well, what I do is pretty straightforward," said Kasey. "For the most part, I stay in the TED* Coach role and practice the principle of 'Ask first, tell second.' And I keep an eye on my learning intention—which is to guide the employee's reflection on their own performance.

"The first step is a form of focusing on the outcome: I ask them for their thoughts on what the expectations are for anyone assigned to their job. In some cases, I will have asked them to review their job description in advance—I might email it to them ahead of our meeting time. Also, I let them know coming into the meeting that we're going to talk about their performance and how things are going, generally.

"So, first I listen to their perceptions of the job expectations. Then I chime in with anything that I think might be missing from their description. Again, it's 'ask first, tell second.'"

"Once we're in alignment about the expectations of the job, I move to current reality. I ask them to share what they think they're doing well, consistent with those job expectations. If what they say sounds on target, I make sure to affirm what they share, and then add my own positive observations."

"That sounds great," said Lucas.

"Yes, so that covers the supports." Kasey went on, "After we've explored what actions or attitudes support the expectations of their job, I'm then going to shift the conversation toward what is inhibiting or getting in the way of the employee meeting those expectations."

"That could be a little tougher," Lucas mused.

"Well, the next step is critical," said Kasey, leaning forward. "I affirm whatever is going well in their work and then say, '*And* we need to explore what isn't going well.' The word *and* is the pivot—I specifically avoid using the word *but*. If I say something positive to you and follow it with the word *but*, that word would negate and diminish all the good things I've just said, right? All you would hear is 'But . . .'"

"I never thought about that," said Lucas, "but I can see your point. Oh, I mean, *and* I see your point."

They both laughed. "Right!" said Kasey.

"So how do you get into what's not working?" said Lucas.

"I ask them another question and get ready to listen to their answer. I ask them to reflect on anything they may be doing—or not doing—that is inconsistent with, or not aligned with, the expectations of their job. If I've set the right tone up to that point, I'm often amazed at how readily people will speak to what isn't going well. And of course, after they've finished speaking, I'm prepared to point out anything that they don't seem to have identified. I try to make sure my tone is objective, rather than having it come across as blame and judgment. If I blamed or judged them, even in my tone of voice, they would immediately see me as a Persecutor, which usually leads to defensiveness.

"So, once we've explored both the supports and the inhibitors in the current reality, I then ask them what they think they need to do to bring their performance in line with the job's expectations. Say, over the next thirty to sixty days. At this point I'm really looking for baby steps that they can commit to."

"Boy, my conversation this morning could have been so much different if I'd used the whole dynamic tension framework," Lucas said thoughtfully. "We did get to a baby step—we agreed that he would come up with a system to prevent the situation from happening again. But again . . . I mean, *and* again . . . what you just described would have been really appropriate. I'll definitely try that next time."

"It doesn't work perfectly 100 percent of the time, of course," Kasey added, "but I've seen it improve the situation more times than it hasn't.

"And one other thing: I make it clear—from a Challenger's learning intention—that I will both support the person I'm talking to in making the changes they've committed to, and I will hold them responsible and accountable for following through on those commitments."

Lucas nodded. "I'm really beginning to see that there are a lot of different ways to, as Ted put it, harness dynamic tension."

The Action Planning Process

"One of the other things we've done in the various customer call center departments is to use the process in our project planning," Kasey said. She took a sip of her coffee. "We've added a fourth step to the three-step dance of dynamic tension that Ted teaches."

"What's the additional step?" said Lucas. He had brought his journal and now opened it, ready to capture any helpful tips.

"Okay, here's an example," said Kasey. "Remember when I told you about the Collections group and how they shifted from a Problem Orientation to an Outcome Orientation in working with customers?"

"I sure do," said Lucas. "That has really stayed with me."

"As you might imagine," Kasey continued, "making that change took a lot of time and planning because all of our systems and processes were designed from the Problem—really, the Victim—Orientation. As a bank, we had assumed a Victim perspective, seeing the customers with past-due accounts as Persecutors who were not honoring their financial commitments to us. The whole approach produced and perpetuated drama with the customers that the Collections Department had to deal with.

"To turn it around, we started using dynamic tension as our action planning process. First we began, as you know you always do, by taking the time to envision our outcome: Collections transforming the way they related to customers. We spent one whole meeting just describing the outcome and how we would know it when we achieved it, both from the bank's perspective and from the customer's experience. We took half a day to do that, and it really turned out to be worth the time and effort."

Kasey continued, "Then we had another meeting where we brainstormed how our systems, processes, and structures already supported us in achieving that outcome, as well as those aspects that were inhibiting our capacity to approach customers in the new way we wanted. We identified a number of problems with our current Collections process that we would need to address."

Lucas looked up from his journal, where he was taking notes. "I'm with you so far," he said.

"The next step we did is the innovation we added to Ted's dynamic tension model. The new step was a little more specific to an action planning process," said Kasey.

"I'm really curious now!" said Lucas, pen poised over his journal.

"Well, here it is: before we moved on to our baby steps," said Kasey, "we brainstormed *possible next steps* we could consider taking action on. We looked at our current reality—both supports and inhibitors—in relation to our outcome. And then we came up with four options about what we *might* do next. Our tag words for these were *keep*, *stop*, *change*, and *start*.

"I'll tell you where we got the idea for each of those. All of the actions we needed to *keep* doing came from the supports list—they were things we needed to keep focused on and continue doing, to support our envisioned outcome. Next we had to identify what actions we could *stop* doing. We found those by taking a close look at the inhibitors list to see if there was anything we were putting time and resources into that wasn't necessary. One obvious one was to stop treating our customers as either Persecutors or Victims.

"Third, we considered what we could *change*, or do

differently. Most of those things were culled from the inhibitors list. But we also noticed a few things that had been going well, and were captured in the supports list, that we could tweak to make even more effective."

Lucas finished writing and held up his hand. "Could you give me an example of one of the things from the supports list that you decided to change?"

"Sure," said Kasey. "We knew that we had in our records the entire history of each customer's relationship with the bank. But we were only using that system to check and see when a customer *stopped* paying. We were ignoring a lot of information that was readily available to us. So as one of the baby steps in this process, we decided to change the way the customer's history was displayed. We did this specifically so we could see if there had been times in the past when the customer had been past due on a payment and yet still managed to make the payment before their account went to the Collections department. That way, we could let the customer know we were aware of this and reinforce with them that there had been other times they fell behind but had ultimately made good on their loan or credit payments."

"Less negative, more affirmative. Got it, thanks," Lucas said.

"Then last, to round out our possible next steps, we brainstormed what we could *start* doing. These were actions related to the outcome that we weren't doing yet. In light of our envisioned outcome, these things were what I call 'conspicuous by their absence'—they were things we could easily see were important to the outcome. One simple example came up in the early planning stage: we could start treating the customers, again, as Creators who probably wanted to keep their credit in good standing."

Kasey continued, "We then used the items we had listed in the keep, stop, change, and start categories to determine our baby steps. To do this, we asked ourselves, 'Which of the items we've identified as possible next steps can we take action on *in the next thirty days*?' Those became our first commitments—the baby steps we would take toward our outcome.

"We then set up a rhythm of meeting every thirty days. First we would report on the results of the baby steps. Sometimes we were making forward progress. And sometimes we learned that certain actions we had thought would work seemed not to be working after all."

"Any breakthroughs?" Lucas asked. "Ted told me that every baby step is either a step forward, a step back, or, at times, a breakthrough."

"That's right," said Kasey. "In this case, over the first few months that we met and worked this dynamic tension process, planning and testing this new course of action with our Collections group, I can't recall a particular breakthrough. But as we gained momentum and started trying out some of our later baby steps, we definitely saw breakthroughs in the results that were emerging. It was pretty exciting."

"I'll bet!" said Lucas. To himself he thought about what a thrill it would be to help lead a process that actually ended up changing the customer's perception of the bank from Persecutor to Challenger or Coach.

Lucas skimmed through the notes he'd written in his journal. "So, just to be sure I understand . . . After you had fully described the outcome with your team, and then assessed the supports and inhibitors that factored into the current reality, you brainstormed your four possible types of next steps—making lists of things to keep, stop, change, or start—before you committed to any specific baby steps."

"You got it, Lucas!" said Kasey. "That's the dynamic tension action planning process." She smiled. "At every meeting, as we worked through the process, we would reconnect to the outcome, to keep it at the forefront of our focus. We would also debrief the results of the baby steps we had taken and see whether those baby steps had made any observable impact on the current reality. Or, when something unexpected arose that we needed to take into account, we would revisit, add to, or revise our possible next steps. Then once again we'd identify and commit to our baby steps for the next thirty days."

Kasey sighed. "It was a huge project and a pretty complex process overall." She smiled. "And yet we completed it in just six months. For such a big transformation, it was really efficient."

"Wow!" said Lucas. "That really is impressive. You must be pretty proud of the way you led your team through that process. It certainly must account for the success you've had here."

"Actually, Lucas, I didn't lead that project," said Kasey.

"The whole process was led by the woman who supervises the Collections Department. I've done my best to share the 3 Vital Questions with my direct report team, and now they use these tools and processes all the time. So the Collections supervisor involved several members of her team and brought in other folks, like IT, when it was relevant. I participated, of course, but when it comes to working this kind of process, I like to, as they say, 'check my stripes at the door.' It was a 'we' process, not a 'me as leader' process."

Lucas closed his journal, leaned back, and sighed. "I could only dream of working in such a great environment. It's really inspiring, Kasey."

"Interesting you should say that, Lucas," Kasey said as she leaned forward to rest her elbows on the table. "Because that gets into the reason I asked you to meet with me. There's a job opening that's going to be posted tomorrow, and it's one I hope you'll consider applying for. It's as supervisor of the team responsible for the Help Desk here in the Customer Call Center."

Lucas had stopped taking notes and listened with increasing interest.

Kasey continued, "While that position reports to me, we take a team approach to the interviewing process here. So, in addition to my conducting interviews, all job candidates are also interviewed by all of the other supervisors who report to me. With what you've learned from Ted, and given the conversations we've had, I think you'd make a good candidate."

Lucas was stunned. It was quite a compliment.

"Also," Kasey added, "I should tell you that I've been considering the fact that we're neighbors and have had these wonderful conversations. So to keep things fair, if you do decide to apply for the position, I would include my boss in the interview process, too. I would rely heavily on his input, along with the input of the team, as to whom we hire."

"Wow," said Lucas. "I sure didn't see that coming. Really, I don't know what to say."

He thought out loud, "I still have that project to develop the analyst report template, although that should be completed in a couple of weeks. So, yes, I think I would like to be considered for the position. I can't thank you enough for giving me the heads up, Kasey." Lucas grinned.

"Good!" said Kasey with a warm smile. "Let's go through the formal process and see how things play out. I appreciate your stopping by late in the afternoon on such short notice."

Lucas stood up, suddenly speechless. He managed to shake Kasey's hand. "Thanks," was all he could think to say.

"Sure thing, Lucas," said Kasey.

A bit dazed, Lucas took the elevator down to his floor and walked down the corridor of cubicles to his office. He sat down and looked at the picture of Sarah, Carson, and Emily as he pondered the possibility of the supervisory position Kasey had described. Supervising the Help Desk would mean he'd need to understand the computer system they used—that was a big part of their process. Lucas's computer science degree was certainly aligned with that need. He hoped the way he had led his data analytics team as a team leader would be a plus in the application process.

Lucas had just shut down his laptop and slipped it into his backpack when he heard the door at the end of the corridor clanging open. "Great!" he thought. "I can't wait to tell Ted about this new development."

Lucas gathered his things and headed for the door. But instead of the friendly face he'd expected, he saw a new custodian standing behind the cleaning cart.

"Hello," said Lucas. "I thought maybe you were Ted. Are you substituting for him on this floor tonight?"

The man barely glanced up from his scan of the cubicles. "Nah," he said. "Ted got transferred. I'm the janitor on this floor now. Gotta keep moving." He swept past Lucas, scooped up the nearest trash can, and emptied it into the bin.

Still, Lucas, found himself grinning as he made his way out to the car for the drive home. So much had happened in the last hour . . . and in the last several months.

Epilogue

It had been well over a year since Lucas had last talked with Ted. So much had happened since then. He wished there were some way to let Ted know about the positive effect of learning the 3 Vital Questions, and of having the awareness to shift from the DDT to TED* in so many situations in his life, at home as well as at his new job.

For starters, Lucas was now sitting at his desk in his new office—an office with a door—having accepted the position of supervisor of the Customer Service Department's online banking Help Desk, leading a team of eight representatives. He was grateful that his computer degree had turned out to be as helpful as he had hoped, but he was even more excited about leading a team of young professionals who treated customers as Creators with an outcome in mind, rather than as Victims oppressed by technology or online banking issues.

When Lucas had given notice to his former boss that he'd applied for the new job, he'd been pleasantly surprised.

His boss had said, "Well, I'll be unhappy to lose you, Lucas, but I can't say I'm surprised you're moving up. I've seen an impressive change in the way you've dealt with challenges on the job these past few months."

Lucas had then shared a little about what he'd learned during those months, especially about being oriented to outcomes rather than problems. He decided not to talk about the FISBEs as Victim and Creator Orientations, but he did show his boss the diagrams he had copied in his journal from his late-night chats with Ted.

The boss had smiled. "Hmm. I can see there's a 'pattern of results' associated with each of these mindsets."

"Yes," Lucas had agreed. "It's been a game changer for the way I approach things."

"Good for you, Lucas," his boss had said. "And good luck. I hope you get it."

And Lucas *had* gotten the job. In the first week, as he'd moved into his new office and began to get acclimated, Lucas gained a deeper appreciation of what Kasey had shared with him about leading the departments. He saw how she had integrated the 3 Vital Questions and the ways of thinking, relating, and taking action that Ted had taught them both. During Lucas's first week on the job, a facilitator from Human Resources took Lucas and his eight team reps through a "new manager assimilation" process that allowed him to really get a sense of the individuals on his team. He heard what was on their minds and was able to give them a look into the mind of their new supervisor as well, by sharing his leadership and management philosophy.

When Lucas shared his approach, he spoke briefly of adopting a Creator Orientation, and expressed his desire that they work together as Co-Creators, Challengers, and Coaches.

"I'd like to harness the dynamic tension between our desired outcomes and our current realities, as our essential action planning process," he said. Then he held his breath for their response. Was he coming on too strong right at the start?

"Wow, I'm so relieved to hear you using the 3VQ language!" one of his new team members said. "We've been using those models, and we all really like how it works to keep things on track and moving."

Lucas later learned that Kasey had made the 3 Vital Questions—3VQ—a standard part of the new-employee orientation. She hadn't asked Lucas to go through it since she knew of his previous familiarity with it, through their mutual friend Ted. Kasey hadn't mentioned that the retail banking group she was responsible for now shared this common language and its frameworks. Even though he had just arrived in his new position, Lucas felt as though he had come home.

That first week, Kasey shared with Lucas a set of commitments used at the start of meetings held in all of her departments. She called them the "Seven Commitments for Empowered Collaboration." Lucas began using the Seven Commitments in his regular weekly meetings with his staff. Unlike the hit-and-run feeling of the huddles he used to have with the data analysts in his previous job, Lucas found these Seven Commitments brought everyone at the meeting into a common focus. And it gave them all a positive reminder about how they had all agreed to conduct their relationships in the department.

Lucas watched his computer screen. The readouts showed him who was on the phone at any given time, while measuring things like how long the call took, what aspect of the online customer experience the call was about, and—if the customer agreed to a short survey at the end of their interaction with the rep—how the customer had rated their experience. Lucas was proud of the fact that the ratings of customer satisfaction were almost always near the top of the scale.

As he reflected back over the year, Lucas cringed as he remembered a few times he'd still gone reactive or defaulted to the Rescuer role with a member of his team or someone from another department. And—hard as it was to swallow—he also recalled how he still sometimes slipped into a Persecutor role, complaining about the rare times when a customer hadn't been satisfied with the support they'd received.

Even in those times, however, the ongoing practice of shifting from the DDT to the TED* roles helped Lucas regain his focus on outcomes and empowered relationships. He often recalled a comment Ted had made:

"The measure of progress is that you catch yourself sooner and make the shift to a TED* role quicker, Lucas. Two steps forward and one step back . . . that's still progress, my friend! This is a daily practice and a lifelong journey."

Leaning back in his chair, Lucas gazed at the whiteboard on the wall, with its two FISBEs of the Victim and Creator Orientations and the triangles of the Dreaded Drama Triangle (DDT) and The Empowerment Dynamic (TED).

On his whiteboard, Lucas had also added the basics of dynamic tension: outcome; current reality; supports and inhibitors; and baby steps.

Kasey had become quite a mentor for Lucas. Of course, that fortunate friendship had actually begun with their serendipitous conversation while waiting for the elevator. Over the past year, as Lucas had begun reporting to Kasey as his manager, he marveled at her ability to be a Coach—most of the time—and to be a Challenger when necessary, too, while they worked together as Co-Creators in evolving the bank's customer experience.

Lucas smiled at the family portrait on his desk, taken in their backyard after a surprise snowfall last winter. Carson was now in the third grade and doing well, and Emily was a budding fifth-grader getting interested in world affairs . . . and boys. As the photographer had taken the picture, Lucas had given Sarah a little squeeze, and his wife had flashed her winning smile. After the photo session was done, she told him how grateful she was that they'd chosen to do their best to raise their children as Creators.

Behind them in the photo was a sharp-looking new fence. Lucas's promotion to his new job had made it possible to have the fence replaced with barely a dent in their savings.

The sound of someone knocking shook Lucas out of his reverie. He looked up. One of his Help Desk reps, Jason, was standing in the open door.

"Got a minute?"

"Of course," Lucas responded. "Come on in. What's up?"

The rep sat down. "I just got off the phone with a customer. I think she was satisfied with the support we gave her. But the call raised an issue that has been coming up again and again these past few weeks. I was wondering if we could come up with a proactive way to prevent those kinds of situations happening in the future?"

Lucas asked a few questions to clarify the issue and to make sure he understood what the rep had in mind. Then he stood up and went to the whiteboard. Lucas picked up a green marker and asked, "Okay then! What's the outcome we want to create?"

Afterword

While the story in this book is a fable, much of what is told here is not fiction. As an employee, as a manager, and as a consultant, I have personally experienced the kind of transformation Lucas experienced.

The fable's setting also comes from my own background. At one point I spent over a decade associated with a large financial services company, where I worked in an office environment divided into cubicles.

One of the most difficult and drama-filled periods of my professional life featured a boss much like the fellow Lucas works for. I am grateful that it was also a time of poignant learning during which I discovered how I wanted to show up—and how I didn't—in the formal manager-leader role I landed in just a few years later. I made the shift from seeing my situation as a "problem" that triggered a habitual reaction, to seeing each situation as an opportunity to clarify what I wanted to create in my professional path.

Today's organizational environments—from businesses to universities to governments—are chock-full of dramas. These range from the daily dramas of disagreement and disgruntlement, to severe bullying and power plays, to the life-threatening events we all see in the news.

While these 3 Vital Questions may not prevent all of this drama, they can definitely transform organizations that use them consistently to deal with daily challenges. I have even seen managers fundamentally shift the way they manage as they come to see the cost of the dramas they have been unwittingly producing or perpetuating.

Our organizations, and indeed, our world, can only benefit from cultivating the transformative capacity of these 3 Vital Questions.

In the work that my wife and partner, Donna, and I do together, we hold this aspiration: that we be Co-Creators collaborating in service to all whom we work with—our customers and clients, our vendors and co-workers, and our communities.

We encourage you to apply these 3 Vital Questions in your workplace, along with the Seven Commitments for Collaboration you'll find at the back of this book. We challenge you, as well, to consider what other areas of your life might be transformed by these simple questions. Only by upgrading our ways of thinking and relating to one another—little by little, day by day—only by taking generative action, can we transform as well as protect what is nearest and dearest to us.

May our actions have a positive impact on the world.

Acknowledgments

So many people have contributed to my journey, in myriad ways. As the work from my first book, *The Power of TED**, with its message of "self-leadership," matured and morphed into a larger expression touching on all areas of life, I have returned to my roots of organizational leadership development. The 3 Vital Questions (aka 3VQ) offer a taste of the wisdom I have been blessed to gain from others along my way, spiced with some personal epiphanies.

No one has influenced my thinking, way of being in the world, and professional expression more than my longtime friend Bob Anderson, founder of The Leadership Circle and co-author of *Mastering Leadership.* Thank you for introducing me to the Problem and Outcome Orientations and for encouraging me to find my own voice and my own ways of expressing them.

To my dear colleagues Bob A., Jim Anderson, Dan Holden, and Barbara Braham, PhD, and to the circle of professional friends who have gathered around tables at the University of Notre Dame while serving as coaches for the Executive Integral Leadership Program—a deep bow of gratitude for your love and support as I faced my own "dark nights" in the DDT and for always affirming the Creator essence we all share.

For many years, the frameworks in TED* (*The Empowerment Dynamic)® were introduced to organizational leaders through the early adopters at the Stagen Leadership Academy: Bert Parlee, Rand Stagen, Paul Landraitis, and Stagen Leadership's many fine coaches and facilitators. The resounding enthusiasm of their clients—who called TED* the "stickiest" part of the powerful Stagen curriculum—provided a big dose of encouragement for me to write a book that both includes and transcends the TED* frameworks while illustrating their application in an organizational setting.

The very first TED* workshop was championed and co-led by Molly Gordon, MCC and Bert Parlee, which led to the emergence of TED* Practitioners.

For ten years, our community of TED* (and now 3VQ) practitioners has cheered us on and taken this work on the road, providing generous feedback, creativity, and inspiring success stories. You all are truly exemplars of a community of practice.

Many thanks go to the first readers of the manuscript: Darryl Greene, Chris Nagel, Barry Rellaford, Tom Womeldorff, Leslye Wood, and McKenzie Zajonc. Your overwhelmingly positive early encouragement, as well as keen observations, contributed much to the final manuscript.

Once again, Ceci Miller has been this work's champion, midwife, editor, publishing consultant, and manager extraordinaire. You and your marketing partner, Carlos Ferreyros, took to the vision of 3VQ from the very start and brought your talents and gifts—as well as encouragement and challenge—together with an incredible team of professionals to produce and promote this book dedicated to "transforming workplace drama."

Thanks to copyeditor Kyra Freestar of Tandem Editing LLC, book designer Bob Lanphear (who has been a major partner in every one of our projects), and indexer Beth Nauman-Montana.

Debbie Hulbert, our director of communications and customer experience, has contributed so much over these ten-plus years, bringing talent, creativity, and a genuine love of TED* to the evolution of our websites, materials, e-course, and so much more.

And finally, this work would never have been born as TED* or matured into the 3 Vital Questions without the partnership of Donna Zajonc, MCC—my dear wife, workshop co-presenter, and director of coaching and practitioner services. You believed in me and this work even when I did not believe in myself. Your vision, passion, and drive has expanded our work into realms of service to individuals, teams, and organizations beyond what either of us could have imagined when we began our journey as husband and wife and Co-Creators. Donna, I love you with all my heart.

Suggested Reading

Anderson, Robert J., and Adam, William A. *Mastering Leadership: An Integrated Framework for Breakthrough Performance and Extraordinary Business Results.* Hoboken, NJ: John Wiley & Sons; 2016.

Anderson, Robert J. "The Spirit of Leadership" and other white papers; https://leadershipcircle.com/whitepapers

Dweck, Carol S. *Mindset: The New Psychology of Success.* New York: Ballantine Books; 2006.

Fritz, Robert. *The Path of Least Resistance: Learning to Become the Creative Force in Your Own Life.* New York: Fawcett Columbine; 1989.

Fritz, Robert. *Creating: A Practical Guide to the Creative Process and How to Use It to Create Anything—a Work of Art, a Relationship, a Career, or a Better Life.* New York: Fawcett Columbine; 1991.

Karpman, Stephen B. *A Game Free Life: The New Transactional Analysis of Intimacy, Openness, and Happiness.* San Francisco: Drama Triangle Publications; 2014.

Kegan, Robert, and Lahey, Lisa Laskow. *How the Way We Talk Can Change the Way We Work: Seven Languages for Transformation.* San Francisco: Jossey-Bass; 2001.

Kegan, Robert, and Lahey, Lisa Laskow. *Immunity to Change: How to Overcome It and Unlock Potential in Yourself and Your Organization.* Boston: Harvard Business School Publishing; 2009.

Senge, Peter. *The Fifth Discipline: The Art and Practice of the Learning Organization.* New York: Doubleday/Currency; 1990.

Senge, Peter. "Building Learning Organizations." *Journal for Quality and Participation* 15, no. 2 (March 1992): 30–39.

Singer, Michael A. *The Untethered Soul: The Journey Beyond Yourself.* Oakland, CA: New Harbinger Publications; 2006.

Would you like to bring the
transformational power of the
3 Vital Questions to your life and work?

Check out your options at
3VitalQuestions.com

Share the Book with Others
Bring 3VQ to Your Workplace
Take a Course with David Emerald

Books by David Emerald

3 Vital Questions
Transforming Workplace Drama

The Power of TED*
(*The Empowerment Dynamic)

Index

Seven Commitments for Collaboration™

by David Emerald

1. **Adopt a Creator Orientation**—We commit to focus our attention on creating outcomes. Passion motivates the actions we take in expressing and manifesting our shared vision. We address problems in service to the accomplishment of our outcomes and increase our capacity to create by learning from each step as we get closer to—and clearer about—our desired outcomes.

2. **Act as Co-Creators**—We are all Creators and commit to work together as partners in creating outcomes. We use hierarchy sparingly and consciously. We harness our individual and collective power to create and support our co-creating as Challengers and Coaches. Our politics are authentic and respectful of the diversity of viewpoints. When things do not go smoothly, we assume innocent intent of others.

3. **Speak to Outcomes**—We commit to be conscious of how we speak and to focus our form of interaction on the purpose and outcomes at hand as we work through issues and opportunities. We balance advocacy for action with inquiry to understand all viewpoints. We are open to being influenced in our deliberations. We use dialogue when we need to deepen our understanding before advocating action.

4. **Challenge Assumptions**—We commit to identify and challenge assumptions—first our own individually and then those of others and the team. We agree to reaffirm and/or revise those assumptions which serve our mission and purpose and to let go of those that inhibit or no longer serve our creating. We periodically review our assumptions.

5. **Listen for Possibility**—We commit to listen to one another openly and generously, seeking always to understand others' viewpoints. We suspend our own assessments and assumptions while listening for the possibilities in others' perspectives.

6. **Harness Dynamic Tension**—We have a bias for action and engage dynamic tension in manifesting outcomes. We clarify our vision and/or outcomes. We identify and leverage supporting and helpful aspects of current reality and solve problems and eliminate inhibitors to our success. We progress by taking "baby steps" that move us closer to our outcomes—and we welcome the breakthroughs and leaps that accelerate our advancement.

7. **Hold One Another Accountable**—We commit to support and hold one another accountable as we adopt these new ways of being and working together. We know growth requires change. We compassionately confront old, outmoded, and unconscious behaviors when they occur, while affirming one another and celebrating when we experience actions that reflect our aspirations.